T0078102

THE
BALOCH
CULTURAL
HERITAGE

JAN MUHAMMAD DASHTI

Trafford
PUBLISHING® www.trafford.com
North America & international
toll-free: 844-688-6899 (USA & Canada)
fax: 812 355 4082

Dedicated
To
The Baloch Youth

CONTENTS

FOREWORD

No culture could achieve any compactness without continuity. The continuity which may be geographical or religious can hardly imply any cultural homogeneity unless people attain a life-pattern inspired by the fundamental values and depicted through its social and political institutions. Any term thus connoting territorial or religious culture like the Asian, the Muslim or Christian culture would be a misnomer. The factors of cultural coherence are common history and traditions which invariably produce a common outlook. In other words, a collective will, generated by common traditions and past glory, would not only unite a people and give meaning to their Culture but also guarantee its vitality and strength. The culture remains vigorous and forceful as long as the people find some real fulfilment by living up to the common values, which are never automatically adopted as a legacy. Every generation must recapture them afresh in view of their usefulness.

This book is a modest effort to discuss the conditions which have ensured the continuity of the Baloch culture, and also the inspiring characteristics which still direct the Baloch society.

Written source material on Baloch history and culture is almost scarce, which save some faint references in a few ancient documents which require a very cautious and scientific analysis for arriving at proper conclusions. Tremendous efforts are needed to separate facts from fiction and distortions of the modern writers on the Baloch. One of the somewhat reliable sources could be the Baloch traditions preserved mostly in classical poetry and folk literature. There also one has to proceed with extra care to avoid the later bardic additions to almost every poem.

Balochi poetry has undergone many changes according to the requirements of the time. We find in the so-called poem of genealogy that Rind, a Baloch tribe, migrated from Aleppo, Syria, after the martyrdom of Hussain, grandson of Prophet Mohammad. There is also a poem indicating that Baloch belonged to the Shia sect of Islam. Both of these poems are far from the truth. Rind suzerainty in Eastern Balochistan for a few Decades led to general desires of every Baloch or indigenous non- Baloch tribe to associate itself with Rind or claim to have been originally Rind. One of the famous Baloch tribes, Lashaar, after their defeat and migration had got some later bardic contempts, and their leaders were ridiculed in order to flatter the Rind and their allies. Some tribes who did not even exist at that period were later mentioned in the poems as participating in Rind-Lashaar Wars. There is an interesting poem on the Battle of Gokprosh, in which Mir Baloch Khan Nosherwani was killed with scores of others. Mehraab Khan, the Gichki sovereign of Kech, who fled from the battlefield with his entire *Lashkar* (army) without a fight has widely been praised for what the poet says his bravery and extreme courage. '*He was the only chief throughout Balochistan, from Bella to Kalat, who decided to fight the British*', the poem narrates. Since Mehraab Khan, after his treacherous act of fleeing the battle, remained the ruler of Kech after evolving an understanding with the alien masters, no one dared to compose a derogatory poem taunting him for his cowardliness and treachery. Similarly, Mir Chaakar's journey to Hirat to seek help against Lashaar, coming out of seemingly impossible tests of bravery like the killing of an elephant, or riding an untamed horse; Hammal, fighting a lion or Beebgr kidnapping the daughter of the King of Kandahar, are merely fictitious or grossly exaggerated stories.

Therefore, in this work, every notion based only on poetic traditions has been checked with available historical records and general geopolitical, the religious, and cultural history of the Baloch as well as the cultural traits of other peoples of this region. As regards folk literature, one has also great difficulty in separating foreign influences from original Baloch folks. I have endeavored to keep all these factors in view while depending on poetry and folk literature when arriving at conclusions.

It may also be pointed out that this book is by no means an attempt to produce a systematic history of the Baloch people. It depicts their culture and traditions. The first chapter which deals briefly with their history and racial origin has been included merely as an introductory part for facilitating the reader in the understanding of the Baloch cultural characteristics in their correct historical perspective.

Balochi poems, proverbs, maxims, etc, have been quoted in footnotes as the source of assertion as well as a further guide to the readers of Balochi literature.

Translation of poetry was the most irksome because the translation of a poem is always difficult in another language. This is due to the fact that the poet always contrives to express exactly what he wants to communicate by employing all the resources of the language, matching the words and phrases and putting them in a beautifully constructed rhythmical order. Special efforts have, however, been made to produce a proper and reasonable rendering of Balochi poems quoted.

Jan Muhammad Dashti
Quetta,
August, 2020

INTRODUCTION

Mr. Jan Muhammad Dashti has gathered sufficient evidence to contest the theory that the Baloch are Semites. Following the history of both the racial groups, the Semites and the Aryans, he has asserted that the Baloch are Aryans and that their original home was the Caspian Sea region. Some resemblances of cultural traits of the Baloch with Semites have been dealt with analytically and regarded as merely the result of contacts of people of the Iranian plateau with Mesopotamians or of Semites in various stages of early history. I have gone through the book. It contains reasonably compelling arguments; a point of view on many of its aspects one may disagree with but the book is nevertheless a masterly account of the Baloch history and culture. I am confident if researches are conducted on the same lines and with the same fairness, it would go a long way in helping to find further clues about the Baloch racial origin.

The history of the Baloch is, however, still in dark. Research scholars have different opinions. Some say they belong to the northern regions of Elburz, now inhabited by Ashkanis, originally Aryans. Some historians maintain that they came from Halab, Aleppo, and are Semites. It is also believed that they are from the old stock of Sumerians of Mesopotamia, while others regard the Baloch as the remnants of the indigenous population of the area. The historians, however, mostly concern themselves in tracing the Baloch racial origin either from among the Indo- Europeans or the Semites. Neither should one object on these methods for historical research nor doubt the fact that there had been an admixture of various people with the Baloch like the Scythians, Parthians, Ashkanis, Sakas, Kushans, Huns, Turks and many other: nor contest the proposition that Baloch, culturally were greatly influenced by Tigris-Euphrates civilization at different stages of history. My point is that there is yet a third source of human civilization which is the main font for the Indus and Tigris-Euphrates civilizations and very nearer to the Baloch. This civilization flourished in Susa around 3500 B.C. Ironically, however, least researches have been conducted on this in the context of Baloch racial origin. Mr. Jan Dashti talks of a very 'remote possibility 'of the Baloch belonging to Elamite tribes. I am sure further research may establish that the possibility is not as remote as presumed by him.

Before the Indo-European and Iranian movements from the Caspian Sea regions and Central Asia, history records another migration which took place a little over 3500 B.C. from the north. Following the routes north of Elburz and through Zagros, these people stopped in the River Qaroon valley. They settled in and around Susa. From there they later on spread towards the west to the fertile valley of Euphrates and to the east up to the Indus. They were, in fact, the founders of the great Sumerian civilization (4300-2371 B.C.) in the west, and Dravidian in the east. History recalls these people as Elamites. The Kingdom of Elam also comprised, besides Susa, the present Iranian provinces of Khuzistan, Kurdistan and the southern parts of Balochistan, along the seashores. Its capital was Susa, The Elamites, later on, conquered Sumer and Akkad and retained them for some time.

I would like to put the following points before the historians writing on the Baloch, for scientific research and analysis in the context of the Baloch racial origin:

i. The non-Semite Sumerians came from the north of Elburz along Kafkaz and entered the Euphrates valley from Bandar ling. The Sumerians and the people of the Indus Valley had elements which belonged to the Mediterranean races. The same people inhabiting Jask were mentioned by the historians, traveling with Alexander of Macedon, as dark-complexioned with curly hair, but different from Negroes. Such people still reside in Balochistan. In Panjgur they are called Nakeeb and Darzada in Kech. Most Indologists believe that there are great similarities between the Dravidian civilization of the Indus and the Euphrates. Tigris civilization of the Sumerians and Balochistan maintained an intermediary link between the two throughout the ancient epochs.

ii. Dravidians came to the Indian subcontinent from Mesopotamia. A small fraction of them stayed in the hills of Makkuran, who were afterward called Brahuis.

iii. The archaeological discoveries in Balochistan, especially the findings at Mehrgad, have reminiscences with the Indus and the Middle Eastern civilizations. If analyzed in a proper historical context, it could be established beyond doubt that the Dravidian and Sumerian civilizations are in fact the product of Elamites, and both had their genesis from Susa.

iv. The Kurds and the Baloch who belong to the same racial group are not part of the Indo-European or Iranian migrations. In my opinion, the Kurds and the Baloch (Brahui) are from the Elam tribes.

v. The Parthian history also confirms the Baloch settlement in the Elburz region. They spoke the same language belonging to Pahlavi, an ancient language of the Parthians. The language they speak now and the customs they follow are closely related to Ashkanis, which is an offshoot of the Parthians. We cannot rule out the possibility that Baloch is originally Parthians and may have mixed up with races like the Sakas and Kushans.

As regards their Semitic origin, no proper evidence has been put forward so far. There appear some links with Mesopotamia which are discernible in culture especially in mythologies. Moreover, the Baloch tribal set-up is closer to Sumerians. This may be because of the proximity of the Baloch with old Mesopotamian tribes. Even if a group of them, for instance, Rind, migrated from Aleppo, they could not be regarded as Semites because all inhabitants of Aleppo were not Semites.

To determine the racial kinship, a close look into the Baloch culture would be imperative. Their customs and traditions have close links with the Central Asian culture, to which the Baloch originally belonged. Take the example of dress. Baloch wears shalwaar, trousers, and turban for the head. Both pertain to the people of Central Asia. From Balochistan to Afghanistan and up to the Kurdish region, in major parts of Central Asia, people wear trousers. Shifting towards Sindh and the Punjab or areas which are part of the subcontinent, the difference is quite clear. Throughout India, Burma and most of the Himalayan regions, *Thehband* is used. Greeks, Chinese, and even

Arabs also wear Turban. The *shalwaar* (Baggy trouser) is the symbol of Baloch culture and distinguishes the Baloch from most other peoples. Similarly, the musical instruments belonging to particular nations are also indicative of their relationship with certain other races. The Baloch possess *thambura* which basically belonged to them; others like the Pathans, the Punjabis and Sindhis do not use it, while the Kurds and Hazara Mongols in Central Asia also use *thambura*. In contrast, the *Saarangi* is shared by all. The typical tuning of Nal which is called nal-o-gul or nal-o-sur, belong to the Baloch only. One performer tunes the Nal while another seconds him. *Naal* is an instrument which is used in reciting epics and a variety of other songs including melodies. Such things and their nature disclose the origin of the Baloch and help to establish links, if any, with peoples of different regions.

No nation or tribe is pure racially. There always exist the chances of blood amalgamation at the various stages of human history. Human groups came together in marriage alliances and kinship. Therefore, it is difficult to say that a particular tribe is invariably related to a certain race or racially pure. For instance, Punjabis do not inherit a singular history. Many outsiders have settled in the area like Gojars. Gojars are living in Balochistan and Iran as well. In Iran they are called Qachars, implying after the word "Gochars", the cattle breeders. Qachars had the previous kingship in Iran which was overthrown by Raza Khan.

The author has touched briefly the archaeological discoveries to assert the proposition that the Baloch have been influenced by many prospering cultures in Balochistan before their settlement. It is fairly evident that the older inhabitants of the region immediately before the Baloch arrival were mostly Jadgaals who spoke a Sindhi dialect. They were predominant in Central Balochistan, especially Jhalawaan, Kalat, and Surab. The Baloch obtained the area from the Jadgaals and drove them towards Lasbela. As for Balochistan; it has the traces of very ancient civilizations. The archaeological discoveries in Nal, Surab, Mehrgad and other places tell the story of ancient men living thousands of years ago. His art of using baked bricks for his dwellings and the architecture is much advanced than that of the present nomads. The Baloch did not have any archetype civilization which the ancient man had. They were surely outsiders. They must have been influenced by the ancient inhabitants in many ways, particularly in religious thoughts and mythologies.

The Baloch and the Brahuis are not two separate peoples, they are one and the same. The only difference is of language. There is absolutely no difference in social practices and the structure of their society. They follow the same customs from birth to death, happiness, and sorrow. It can be said that Brahui philology may be composed of some Median dialects or greatly influence from some Dravidian tongue. Some Indologists believe that Dravidians did come from Mesopotamia; first, they settled in eastern Iran and Makkuran and then proceeded to the Indus Valley. Others firmly believe that they were the ancient population of Balochistan and some parts of the subcontinent, and slowly moved towards west up to Mesopotamia, and east up to the Indus.

The Baloch came to Balochistan in three major groups. The first wave settled in Sistan and was called Naaroi, followed by Brahui who settled in Turan which is nowadays called Jahlawaan. The last was of Rind. Some say Rind is a Balochi word, *"Rand or Randi"* meaning the last; the tribe, therefore, derived its name from the above-mentioned word. The Brahuis and the Baloch lived side by side in Sistan; where still live many Brahui tribes. The latecomers penetrated into Sindh and Punjab. The Baloch migration into Sind was in two waves: from Balochistan and from Punjab. Those who went directly from Balochistan speak Balochi or Sindhi, while those who migrated from Punjab and settled in Sind speak Saraiki, whose remnants are Talpurs, Lagharis and some of the Jathuis.

It is absolutely incorrect to say that Brahuis, including the Mengals who are wrongly presumed to be Mongols, are Dravidians. They, like Balochi speakers, are Aryans. As regards Mengals, they might be the remnants of the Min tribe which once lived in Iran. Further researches may establish a relation between the Iranian Mins and our Mengals. As to their difference in Language, Jan Dashti has rightly asserted that language is not the only criteria for resolving the question of racial kinship. I believe that anyone can adopt any language. For instance, the Baloch in Punjab speaks Saraiki. The Baloch might have learned the Brahui language from some of the old tribes who were once occupying these regions. We cannot even claim that Balochi is the original language of the entire Baloch people. It is possible that they adopted this language after their migration from the Caspian Sea region or they had their original language Brahui either. Another strange phenomenon is that Brahui speakers are called Baloch and

Rakhshaani in Afghanistan. As regard Balochi, it is mentioned in the 4th volume of the Cambridge History of Iran that Balochi is from the Pahlavi language group which was itself a Parthian branch of Indo-Iranian Language, spoken among people of the north −east of Elburz. It is an ancient Aryan language family, the mother − tongue being Sanskrit. Almost all the inhabitants toward the north from Naal to Quetta are Brahui speaking while in the south, toward Kerman, the overwhelming majority speak, Balochi: and in many areas of this plateau, even some of the original Brahui tribes do not know Brahui. In Makkuran, up to Zahidan Balochi speakers are predominant. Brahui is also called Kurdi or *Kurd Gaali*.

It would not be wrong to assert that the Kurds are the cousins of Baloch. The one-third of Mazaari Baloch are kerd or Kurd, who hold Sardari in Balochistan. The Kurds say Baloch are from them, whereas the Baloch also claim that. I cannot say which of the tribe is older or which one is the mother − tribe, but I believe they are one and the same people. The Baloch do not meet the Kurds geographically. They live in the Middle East divisible among Iraq, Turkey, Syria, and Iran. The Kurds themselves seldom meet each other across any country's borderland.

The Baloch live in Pakistan, Iran, and Afghanistan. Triple are their neighbors, which divide the Baloch land and population. Iranian Baloch resides from Mand to Kerman and then downwards from Bandar Abbas to Jiwani along the seashores, occupying approximately 400 miles. From Jiwani up to Karachi some 350 miles along the Arabian Sea, are the Baloch areas with Pakistan. To the northeast from Helmand to Sistan and then toward Zabul is the Baloch territory. The Baloch are, however, densely populated in the Pakistani province of Punjab. Nearly forty thousand Baloch live in USSR. But they are not the permanent settlers. They are nomads.

Frontiers of Balochistan end at Quetta, and there was no further extension. The adjacent territory of Pakhtuns, now in Balochistan, was a part of the Afghan province of Kandahar. It was subjugated and annexed into the British Empire subsequently. Quetta called Shaalkot, was a tehsil under the Khanate.

Balochistan has been a part of Iranian plateau but not of the subcontinent or Indus Valley. This is rather proved by the peculiar inhabitants of the region, their culture, and history. However, one thing is certain that Sind and Balochistan have very cordial relations from time immemorial. Our people have been fascinated by Sindhi culture and vice versa. There has been a natural alliance between Sindh and Balochistan because of history and economy. They developed harmonious ties. There had been trading between them. Traces of Hindu culture are visible in Balochistan mostly through Sindhi influences. Some time back, I found a vessel piece in Naal decorated with a figure of Hanuman on one face, and harna on the other. Till the time of Chach bin Silach, this area, and especially Makkuran, was under Sind; whence some people around Baho-Dashtiari near Kerman are of Sindhi origin; many of them still speak a Sindhi dialect. The archaeological discoveries in Balochistan tell about deep – linking culture with Amri and Mohenjodaro.

The tribal society has to pass through various stages of development. Its economy is pastural and the tribal groups do not restrict themselves to particular areas; rather move in search of pastures or leave places because of congestion or to save the animals from diseases. Migration has been a permanent feature of tribal life. Such people living in an area always share the struggle to provide protection to their animals from drought and diseases and from the hostile forces. Such phenomenon creates a harmonic relationship in shaping the culture of the tribes. Each tribe shares some uniform characteristics. They are allied as well as involved in feuds. They are united when there is danger from outsides and fight each other when the danger is averted. Such is the permanent nature of the tribes.

The tribe was composed of many sub-tribes. It was a sort of federation, the form of which still prevails. Take, for instance, the Bizenjo tribe, to which I belong. It is a federation of Hammalani, Tamrani, Umrani, and Siapaad. The federation is constituted of units which are independent internally and headed by their respective Sardars; below is the line of headmen. These units form the Bizenjo tribe. Each Sardar is empowered to settle disputes of his own faction: whereas disputes among various sections are resolved by the Chief of the entire tribe. If any conflict arises between, for instance, Umrani and Siapaad, it is settled by the Bizenjo Chief, who is always a Hammalani. This is an age-old federation going back to six hundred years or more. Similarly, Rind and Lashaar were not two different people or tribes, as presumed by many people. Both were one and the same under the leadership of Mir Jalalaan. Disputes among them arose when they migrated to Kolwah from Kech. At this juncture, they were divided into two factions. Mir Chaakar became the Sardar of Rind and Mir Gwahraam of Lashaar. I think such a division was quite natural because when the tribe expands numerically: it always splits into many factions, for that is but inevitable. It would simply become difficult to keep the tribe into a single structure for political as well as economic reasons. Therefore, bigger tribes generally fragmented into two or more units. However, what is unfortunate is that the Rind and Lashaar, soon after their division, engaged in a futile war against each other with disastrous consequences which both had to bear.

The Sardari was not obnoxious at the beginning. It was a pressing requirement. It would surely continue in the societies which are undeveloped and remain in the tribal set-up. In such societies, if Sardari is done away with without any proper replacement, anarchy would prevail, and the people would have to carry on without law and administration.

The Sardars were elected Chiefs of the tribes. They were much democratic in their outlook and manners. Disputes were always settled in an open Diwaan where each of the participants had the right to speak and dissent. Efforts were always made for a settlement of conflicts between the parties. The Sardar always followed the majority opinion. Under the Sardari, lands were jointly owned. The Sardars never collected land rent except for the land they owned. The people gave a double share of land to the Sardar for his Sardari and for catering to the expenses of his hospitality. He then had no other claim on the land of the tribe. The land allotted to him as the Sardari land was a non-distributable share.

The British rulers gave special privileges to Sardars as a class who consequently became mini-despots. Otherwise, in the Baloch culture, the Sardar was checked in many ways. He was criticized in the open meetings if he behaved against the accepted norms. The present status of the Sardar is more like a feudal Jagirdar. The social ties and bonds of brotherhood, once characteristic of tribal society, have long been broken. The Sardar previously was never regarded as a superman. If you asked a tribal Bizenjo living in the mountains about his identity he would certainly say he was the brother of so and so, after the name of his Sardar. This reflects the kind of society and equality of status among the Baloch in primitive times.

Kalat was not merely a style of government; rather a State headed by the Khan and based on the tribal confederacy. Some tribes, e.g.

Mari and Bugti, were independent in the same manner the tribal areas now enjoy a sort of autonomy within Pakistan. Lasbela was a mini State within the Khanate and was ruled by a Sardar. Kharan and Makkuran were independent Sardaris. State structure was like a tribal confederacy, and units within the state framework were autonomous and sovereign. All disputes were usually settled by the Sardars except the cases of more complicated nature which were forwarded to Jirga under the Chairmanship of the Khan. Such Jirgas were held twice a year. The Khan had the prerogative of appeal and mercy. It is worth mentioning that the Jirga or joint Jirga is a later phenomenon introduced by the British rulers. In a Baloch social set-up, disputes were resolved through mutual consultations among various factional heads. Only complicated cases were sent to the Khan for adjudication.

The Baloch do not have a caste hierarchy like the Hindus, however, they are very much conscious about ranking in society. This division is strange and improper. In ancient epochs, those who participated in wars were ranked superior, while others who concerned themselves with occupational matters were considered low and employed as servants. We use the word "Lodi" which has been a downtrodden faction in relations to others. Lodis had never been a different caste. They belonged to the same tribe which had many occupational groups who included carpenters, blacksmiths, singers, and other crafts and craftsmen. Luhr is part of Kurds. There was a territory in Iran by the name, Luristan. Luristan may have some bearing on the word "Lodi". In the chivalry period, the family, clan or tribe who were brave fighters and powerful enough to subdue others, were considered superior and usually owned vast areas as fiefs.

Slavery was in vogue among the Baloch, especially in Lasbela and southern Balochistan. Slaves were brought from Africa and purchased by wealthy people. It may be mentioned that Darzada is not the descendants of slaves. They are an old race which existed at the time of Alexander's campaigns. The Greek historians mentioned this strange race, a Mediterranean people, black in complexion. They were tillers of land and peace-loving people.

Unlike most other writers on the Baloch, Jan Dashti has viewed the tribal society and its political and social structure with historical understanding. This is appreciable. The author's analysis of the Baloch culture and traditions should provide a sound base for further inquiries and research. Being a Baloch himself, he has approached the entire cultural structure with understanding and without least prejudices. His chapter on culture gives a fascinating reading for the Baloch and non-Baloch, both alike. In this connection, I would like to add that the Baloch are more sophisticated than any nomadic people. A Baloch who may have spent his life in the mountains never visited a city and has not experienced the journey of a bus or a train is very much civilized when he talks. His rationale behavior and his secular attitude towards religion give the feeling that the Baloch had been related to an advanced culture and civilization in ancient times. He is liberal in religious outlook. Even a single tribe is divided into two or more religious groups with somewhat different practices, but this has never strained relations among the people. Take the example of Zikris. The founder of the sect was Muhammad Junpuri, who was against Emperor Akber's new faith, Din-e-Elahi. It was basically the Mahdavi movement. *Zikris* are very much similar to those of *Numazi*. There are instances where one brother in the same family is a Zikri and another is a Numazi.

The Baloch Cultural Heritage is a valuable contribution towards understanding the Baloch traditions in their proper historical perspective. The author appreciably does not deal with mere events but puts them to critical analysis and interpretations to draw logical conclusions on various aspects of Baloch culture. Although at times, one may get the impression that he has avoided detailed review of quite a few controversial points, the book nevertheless is a masterly treatise which reveals the author's deep intellectual curiosity, scholarship, and resourcefulness.

Mir Ghous Bakhsh Bizenjo

ONE

INTRODUCTION

Culture can be defined as an integrated system of institutions, ideas, customs, and social behavior of a particular people or society. Through cultural elements, a social group interacts. Culture is an important factor in shaping the identity of a people.

The nation as the result of interactive processes involves all who feel a sense of community and express it on a regular basis. It has cultural significance. It is a community of people who have a common historical memory, who reflect common values, and who believe in a common, shared destiny. Nationhood is, therefore a cultural concept. Different cultures can be identified according to a preconceived set of national characteristics.

The national identity has been defined as a process that is always being reconstituted in a process of becoming and by virtue of location in social, material, temporal and spatial contexts. As identity is not fixed, the points of identification continuously move through different nexuses, and these nexuses proliferate through contact, cultural influences, and mobilities. National Identity represents the socio-historical context within which culture is embedded and the means by which culture is produced, transmitted and received.

The feeling that makes a distinction between themselves and others at a collective and individual level expresses and embodies itself in the sense of national identity which has been conceptualized by sociologists as the feelings of a group of people of being a nation and having the feature of continuity that can be transmitted through generations. Throughout history, the nation has been a focus for identification and a sense of belonging. In the process of finding out by a group of people that who they are, they use resources of history, language, and culture. In other words, national identity is the feeling of a people as cohesive whole manifested by distinctive socio-cultural traditions, history, language and inhabiting a region. It is a socially constructed phenomenon resulting from shared symbols, common language, common historical past, common descent.

The need for individuals to feel that they belong to a wider collective group, whether defined as a family, social group or nation is one of the tenets of national identity. The desire of an individual for national membership motivates collective social adhesion. The collective elements of a national identity comprised of beliefs, values, assumptions, and expectations. They are transmitted to members of a nation through the process of socialization. On an individual level, depending on how much the individual is exposed to the socialization process. Therefore, the collective elements of national identity become important parts of an individual's perception of who he or she is. These factors define the self and how members of a community view the world and their own place in it.

The Baloch national identity, in the true sense, began to take shape in early medieval times during a period of increased political and social turmoil in the Iranian Plateau. It was the period when various nationalities tried to assert themselves politically after the collapse of Umayyad and Abbasid dynasties. For the Baloch, it was a time of hardships as they confronted various newly emerging powers. Consequently, they faced genocide and were in constant movement from Kerman to north, east and south of Iranian Plateau in order to escape total annihilation. Although, the Baloch suffered physical, psychological and political setbacks during 11th, 12th, and 13th centuries; nevertheless, despite all sufferings, the migrations and diffusion of the Baloch tribes into various regions, the foundation of the Baloch national identity as a people with its language, and socio-cultural traditions were made. It was the period when the Baloch tribes became dominant over the indigenous groups in present regions which comprised contemporary Eastern or Western Balochistan. With the predominance of the Baloch in these regions, the area was given the name of Balochistan and made a province of the Seljuq empire.

For sociologists, the question of national identity which differentiates peoples, nations, and communities from each other, has been one of the core issues. For Benedict Anderson, national identity is construed and sustained in cultural texts. Here, a nation exists as more than a composite of necessary characteristics, a common people, a common language, a common history, a common territory. "It is imagined because the members of even the smallest nation will never know most of their fellow-members, meet them, or even hear of them, yet in the minds of each lives the image of their communion". Sociologist Smith observed that the underlying functions of national identity include: transcending oblivion through posterity, the restoration of collective dignity through an appeal to a golden age; the realization of fraternity symbols, rites, and ceremonies, which bind the living to the dead and fallen of the community.

Who is a Baloch? What is meant by being a Baloch? The answers to these questions had helped the Baloch to survive difficult times in their national history. For the Baloch, cultural heritage has been a tool of survival throughout history. The cultural traditions are part of general Baloch makeup, had always been with them and as much part of 21st century Baloch as they were in ancient times.

Language is intrinsic to the expression of culture. It is the means by which culture and its traditions and shared values are conveyed and preserved. Language has always a symbolic identity building significance for a specific group or a national entity. Political resistance has adopted the linguistic method to express itself. Balochi language is, without a doubt, a fundamental component of Baloch identity. It interlocks with national identity in other subtle ways. It mirrors the soul of the nation.

Territory or homeland is the means through which a nation will fulfill its destiny. After hundreds of years of migration, when they finally settled in regions which comprised present-day Balochistan, the land became one of the identifying elements of the Baloch. Contemporary Balochistan (the land of the Baloch) that emerges during the 12th century, in its origin, became a space fought for and contested. National land is a basic component of 'national identity', which partly explains why for the last many hundreds of years, the Baloch are so easily mobilized when their territory is threatened, or perceived to be under threat. In this perspective, patriotism pervades the entire Baloch Socio-cultural approach.

A myth can be an erroneous belief but widely shared. They are explanatory narratives, tales that try to explain how the world has come to be, how nature's forces change, or how human actions are ordained by gods and supernatural entities. Myths point to the origins, offering explanations of how something came into being. Legends of gods and heroes play powerful roles in the cultural attitude of a people. Myth is inextricably linked with the concept of national identity. Although, most nations are products of inter-ethnic integration; the myth of common ancestry among the Baloch is critically important. The Baloch typically view their nation as an extended family related by common ancestry, although this belief in a common ancestor is based more on myths and legends. The myth of common ancestry, nevertheless, makes the Baloch as a nation that is natural and eternal.

Race and nation are two mutually exclusive terms with a different meaning. A race will have certain genetically inborn physical features in common, while a nation has common socio-cultural attributes and strong desire to achieve given political objectives. Race cannot be determined on speech classification. Speakers of various languages may form one racial group while people belonging to one race may speak a different language. The case of the Baloch, the Kurd are two distinct people but they belong to the same racial stock. While the Baloch as a nation speaks so many languages (Brahuis, Seraiki, and Balochi) but belong to the same racial stock. The Ugandan tribe Amba speak two different languages but they are considered as one people.

The race has been in a continuous state of transformation. New genes have been introduced by explorers, conquerors and a variety of others. Thus, the notion of purity of race or blood appears to be untenable in view of the vast inter-mingling of peoples throughout history. Movement of the population in prehistoric as well as historic epochs with apparent free interbreeding have resulted in admixtures of various groups.

There are divergent views among scholars regarding the racial origins of the Baloch. An Assyrian, Turco-Iranian and Aryan and even Semitic origin have also been mentioned by many writers. To a certain extent, the origin and etymology of the name Baloch are still obscure. Some believe that it is derived from Median language as Brza-Vaciya from brza-vak, loud cry, in contrast to namravak, quite polite way of talking. While some maintained that the word Baloch is made of two Sanskrit words, Bal and och. Bal means strength or power and och high or magnificent; while some are in the opinion that the word is a nickname meaning a "cock's comb" citing a 17th-century Persian dictionary, Burhan-e- Katih. Baloch troops fought for Astyages or Kai

Khusrau (585-550 BC) were wearing helmets with cockscomb crest, they got the nickname of the Baloch. While listing the warriors of Kai Khusrau, Firdausi in his famous Shahnama, mentioned the Baloch under the command of General Ashkash as follows:

> 'Next (after Gustaham), came shrewd Ashkash, endowed with prudent heart and ready brain. His troop was from the wanderers of the Koch and Baloch with exalted cockscomb crests and very rams to fight. No one had seen their backs in battle or one of their fingers bare of armor. Their banner was a Pard with claws projecting. Ashkash felicitated Kai Khusrau at large upon the happy turn of fortune.'

Studies in the linguistic and cultural history of the region have now established that the Baloch belonged to the migrating Aryan tribes from Central Asia who began dominating Iranian Plateau three thousand years ago. Authentic works on Balochi language has established beyond doubt that it is a member of the northwestern group of Iranian languages, along with Zazaki Kurdish, Gilaki, Mazandarani, and Talyshi, places Balochi among the transitional Western Iranian languages, categorizing it as a group in the sense of being a third member in between North and Southwestern Iranian languages. Persian, Balochi, and Kurdish share common phonetic isoglosses and the speakers of these three languages might once have been in closer contact geographically and ethnically. On cultural grounds, the Baloch share most of the traditions of the Parthian and Medes tribes. Parthian history also confirms the settlement of a people speaking a similar language of Ashkani (Parthian) in the Elborz Mountains and some of the cultural aspects of the Parthian very much indicate close affinities of the Baloch with the Parthians.

Dr. Naseer Dashti's book "The Baloch and Balochistan: a historical account from the beginning to the fall of the Baloch state" presents the theory of Baloch being the inhabitants of Achaemenid Empire's Balashakan province in the western Caspian region. He observed that aspect of the meaning of word 'Baloch' that could have been important in finding the origin of the Baloch had, strangely, been missed by all scholars and researchers. During Achaemenid period, an ethnic group in the name of Balashchik (Balascik) was living alongside many other ethnic entities in the ancient land of Balashagan

(Balashakan) between the Caspian Sea and Lake Van in the present day Turkey and Azerbaijan.

Various rock inscriptions by different Achaemenid Emperors mentioned a region called Balashagan/Balashakan under their rule. There is also mentioning of a people called Balascik living in that region. The Achaemenid Emperor Darius I (Xerxes I 550-486 BC) in the inscriptions proclaimed that they are "king of lands holding many or all peoples". For naming the lands, they used the word Dahyus and Balashagan was one of the Dahyus. During the Sassanid era, Balashagan/Balashakan 'the country of the Balas' was a satrapy of the Empire. It was listed among the northwestern and Caucasian provinces amongst them Albania, Atropatene, Armenia, Iberia, Balashagan, and the gate of Alans was mentioned. The inscription of Sassanid Emperor Shahpur I (240-270 AD) at Naqsh-e-Rostam describes the satrapy of Balashagan as "extending to the Caucasus mountains and the Gate of Albania (Gate of the Alans).

> "And I [Shahpur I] possess the lands [provinces; Greek ethne]: Fars [Persis], Pahlav [Parthia], Huzestan [Khuzistan], Meshan [Maishan, Mesene], Asorestan [Mesopotamia], Nod-Ardakhshiragan [Adiabene], Arbayestan [Arabia], Adurbadagan [Atropatene], Armen [Armenia], Virozan [Iberia], Segan [Machelonia], Arran [Albania], Balasagan up to the Caucasus and to the 'gate of the Alans' and all of Padishkwar[gar] the entire Elburz and Gelan, Mad [Media], Gurgan [Hyrcania], Marv [Margiana], Harey [Aria], and all of Abarshahr [all the upper (=eastern, Parthian) provinces], Kerman [Kerman], Sakastan, Turgistan, Makuran, Pardan [Paradene], Hind [Sind] and Kushanshahr all the way to Pashkibur [Peshavar?] and to the borders of Kashgaria, Sogdia and Chach [Tashken] and of the sea-coast Mazonshahr [Oman]."

Strabo in Book II of his geography gave one of the earliest accounts of the region and mentioned the kingdom of Atropatene that incorporated Balashakan. Strabo mentioned that the monarch of Balashagan also gained the title of King under Sassanid Emperor Ardashir, which most probably would indicate him being a vassal of Sassanid Emperor. Arab historian Ebn Kordabeh mentioned that the King of Balashagan (Balashajan Shah) among the dynasts who received the title of king from Emperor Ardashir. This would indicate that the king of Balashagan had made an act of submission and allegiance to Emperor Ardashir (or to Emperor Shahpur), of whom he became, by the same act, a vassal. According to Shahpur's inscription, most of Transcaucasia was included in his empire, and in the inscription made by Kerdir at the same site it is also proudly mentioned that:

> *'the land of Armenia, Georgia, Albania, and Balashagan, up to the Gate of the Albanians, Shahpur, the king of kings, with his horses and men pillaged, burned and devastated.'*

The heart of Balashakan was the Dasht-e-Balashakan "Balashagan plain," which is virtually identical with the Mogan steppe. According to Ebn Kordabeh, this plain was located on the road from Barzand to Vartan (Vartanakert).

From the ancient Persian accounts, the presence of the Baloch in the region, which was known as Balashagan can be observed from the accounts of the protracted conflict between Kai Khusrau and Afrasiab. It has been established from the Shahnama that the Baloch were under the command of General Ashkash during this period and General Ashkash according to various accounts from Shahnama and from other historical accounts of Iran at that time was deputed to make war on the Turanian territory of Khwarezm. Khwarezm is adjacent to the region which was known at that time as Balashagan.

Strabo provided the names of some tribes that populated Caucasian Albania, including the regions of Artsakh and Utik. These were Utians, Mycians, Caspians, Gargarians, Sakasenians, Gelians, Sodians, Lupenians, Balash [ak] anians, Parsians and Parrasians. Deliberating on these ethnic entities, Hewsen observed that these tribes were certainly not of Armenian origin, and although certain Iranian peoples must have settled here during the long period of Persian and Median rule, most of the natives were not even Indo-Europeans. There is also mention of a Kingdom of Sanesanan whose king during the reign of Armenian King Khusrow II, according to Thomas de Marga, also ruled over other peoples, among whom figured the Balashchik. Having invaded Armenia, the army of this king was cut to pieces by the Armenians; the survivors fell back toward the country of the Balashchik. It would seem then that, toward 335-36

AD, the Massagete king Sanesan occupied a part of Balashagan, where he recruited troops, all the while recognizing, at least nominally, the suzerainty of the King of Kings of Iran.

According to Baladhuri, in the period of early Arab conquests, Balashagan spanned the vast plain extending across the lower course of the Aras (Araxes) river, from Barda'a through Baylaqan to Vartan, Bajarvan, and Barzand. It included the provinces of Arran and Mogan.

It is to this period of history that the original development of the Balochi language can be assigned, which according to linguists is a northwestern Iranian language. This language became the most obvious symbol of the Baloch national identity in the coming centuries. The word Baloch is most probably a rather small modification of term Balascik. There is not much difference in the pronunciation of Balascik, Balashchik, Baloachik, or Baloch. Even today, in different parts of Balochistan, many people call the Baloch as Balochuk and Balochi as Balochiki. It is most probable that the group of the tribe who were living in Balashakan was named after the region or the region itself was named after its inhabitants, the Balascik. The theory of the Baloch coming from Balaschik although appears more logical than the others needs further research and explorations.

The Baloch appear to have been in constant conflict with their neighbors. One of these conflicts might have been the cause of the mass migration of the Baloch from their original inhabitants of Balashagan. The first organized attack on them on a large scale came from the Persian monarch Khusraw I, the Anushervan (531-578 AD), around 531 AD. It seems that the first Baloch migration from Kerman and Sistan toward the east started generally in the early sixth century AD after the Iranian thrust into their region during the reign of the Anushervan. The inroads of Ephthalite Turks into northern Iran might be another factor. After a period of many hundred years, the mention of the Baloch appears in the Arab chronicles after the advent of Islam. The Arab writers of 8th and 9th centuries mentioned the Baloch as Koch o Baloch. Both are considered to be one people, with two names being synonymous. Hudud al Alam localizes the Kufij or Koch in the south-eastern mountainous region of Iran. Nizamul Mulk in Sistan Nama refers to the Kufij and maintains that they lived in the neighborhood of Kerman. The Arab writer Al Istakhri says the Kufij lived on the eastern fringe of the Kerman mountains, which he terms Jabal al kufs. Masudi and ibn Haukal likewise refer to Koch and Belus inhabiting the mountainous fringe of Kerman. The Koch was said to be divided into seven tribes with a different language from the Baloch. It is possible that the Brahuis might have been regarded as Koch.

The Arab rulers of Iran fought occasional battles with the Baloch to keep the trade routes open through Baloch territories of Kerman and Sistan and also keep Baloch influence in their areas to a minimum. However, the Baloch conflict with various regional powers in Iran after the collapse of Arab power during the 10th century caused the migration of many Baloch tribes from Kerman and Dasht regions further towards south and East. Their migration eastward may also have been the result of pressure from the Seljuk invasion in the eleventh century and the devastating inroads later by Genghis Khan. With waves of migrations, by the 11th century, the majority of the Baloch were settled in the present day Balochistan.

17th century Balochistan has been defined as a country between the Arabian Sea and Afghanistan, Sindh, and Persia. The Indian Viceroy, Lord Curzon, defined the Baloch country as the area between the Helmand and its basin that is Farah, Chakansur, Germsel, and Shorawak and Badghis in Hirat to the Arabian sea: and between Kerman and Sindh. Balochistan was divided after the British occupation in 1839. Half of its territory was given to Iran, Eastern Sistan (Nemroz) was included in Afghanistan while the remaining areas came under the control of the newly created country of Pakistan in 1947 and 1948. Iranian Balochistan is generally defined as a region southeast of Iran comprising the province of Sistan wa Balochistan and parts of Kerman and Hormuzgan provinces. There are various estimates regarding the number of Baloch people ranging from 35 to 40 millions throughout the world.

This book is an exploration into the socio-cultural traditions of the Baloch which throughout history became the surviving tools for them as a people against the onslaught of powerful powers of the region.

Regarding the origin of the Baloch, several theories have been put forward by various writers and researchers. They postulated that Baloch is the indigenous inhabitants of present-day Balochistan; the Baloch are Semitic, or the Baloch were part of Central Asian tribes who migrated and settled in the Iranian plateau. Physical traits or biological growth; language; folklore and literature; religion and mythologies; social and political institutions; cultural affinity; geography and history are important factors in determining a people's racial or ethnic origin. With the analyses of these factors, it became clear that there is no resemblance of the Baloch with Semites, although, the Baloch might have assimilated some of their linguistic and societal values. Their linguistic and cultural affinity with Persians and Kurdish give much credibility to the theory that they belong to those groups of tribes who migrated from central Asia some three thousand years ago. They belong to the family of tribes who was speaking Indo-European (Aryan) languages. Chapter two is a discussion on various theories regarding the racial origin of the Baloch.

Culture influences human behavior in a variety of ways. A separate national identity is quite inconceivable without cultural existence. As a sustaining and inspiring force, culture has living ideas. It is deeply rooted in customs, traditions, manners, laws, institutions, beliefs, and rituals, modes of worship and likes and dislikes of a community. The Baloch had some peculiar cultural traits and social ethos. As an individual, a Baloch is highly egoistic and deeply proud. Truthfulness, honesty, keeping one's vows and avenging an injustice were the cherished cultural values among the Baloch. Chapter three is a detail discussion on the socio-cultural values, aspiration, and spirit of the Baloch as a people.

Religion has its domain in a series of human conduct. It is deeply ingrained in culture, traditions, morality, law, and philosophy. Religions or mythologies are experiences, ideas, teachings, and ritual practices, which characterize a human being and his conduct as good or bad, holy or unholy, virtuous, or unvirtuous, godly or ungodly. Historically, the religious beliefs of a people were exploited for political gains, however, the Baloch were never incited in the name of religion. The Baloch are not irreligious but instead of religious or mythological sentiments, they always promptly responded to the call in the name of their culture and traditions. Chapter four deals with religious and mythological beliefs of the Baloch.

The Baloch political system revolved around tribalism. A tribe was a union of many families and clans. Tribalism functioned under Sardari system which served as the institution which offered individual freedom to a Baloch as long as his personal interests did not contradict the interests of the community as a whole. Before the occupation of Balochistan by the British in 1839, Sardars were selected among the best of the individuals in a tribe. In a way, the Baloch political system under tribalism was a form of meritocracy. Formation of tribal unions was important for the survival of the Baloch against the onslaught of powerful forces and ultimately manifested itself in the establishment of the first Baloch state of Kalat in medieval times. Chapter five is an exploration of the political system of the Baloch.

Chapter six comprised of concluding remarks on the cultural heritage of the Baloch.

TWO
THE BALOCH

Because of the lack of any documented historical and anthropological data, the origin of the Baloch as an ethnic entity has been subject to speculations and guesswork. Different views have been put forward. The Baloch being the indigenous inhabitants of present-day Balochistan, the Baloch being Semitic, or the Baloch being the part of central Asian tribes who migrated some three thousand years ago and settled in the Iranian plateau, has been the focus of academic discussions. However, the linguistic, cultural, and geographical factors strongly suggest that the Baloch were part of the migrating tribes who spoke Indo-European languages. Their linguistic and cultural affinity with Persians and Kurdish give much credibility to this theory.

The Baloch

Herzfeld believes that it is derived from brza-vaciya, which came from *brza-vak*, a Median word meaning a loud cry, in contrast to *namravak*, quiet, polite way of talking.[1] Some writers maintain that the Baloch owe their name to Babylonian King, 'Belus', also the name of their God. It is also said that the word is a nickname meaning a 'cock's comb. As the Baloch forces who fought against Astyages (585-550 B.C.) wore distinctive helmets decorated with a cock's comb, the

---

1   E. Herzfeld, Zoroaster and His World, Vol. II, quoted by Yu, V Gankovsky: the peoples of Pakistan, Nauka, Moscow,1971, p.144.

name 'Baloch' is said to have been derived from the token of cock[2]. Some writers believe that etymologically it is made of two Sanskrit words, 'Bal' and Och.' Bal means strength or power, and 'Och' high or magnificent[3]. Yet another erroneous version is that Baloch means 'nomad' or wanderer. This has been presumed perhaps due to the innocent use of the word for nomadic people and maybe because of the fact that the term is used by indigenous settlers for the Baloch nomads. Dr. Naseer Dashti postulated that the word Baloch is the modified form of original Balaschik who were the inhabitants of the Balashkan province of the Achaemenid Empire.

The Baloch migrations

Throughout recorded history, people wanted resources to feed their expanding population and supplement their exhausting resources either through war or mass migration. The Greek expansion after 750 B.C. to the Mediterranean regions and eastwards through Persia and India; and Roman expansion, too, could be analyzed to have been prompted by similar considerations. Byzantine and Iranian empires were also guided by national exigencies of providing greater means to their peoples. On many occasions, the subjugation and forced dispersion of unruly tribes and nations became imperative for the implementation of the expansionist designs of superpowers of the day. Baloch might have been among the victims of such phenomena.

The first Baloch migration from the western Caspian Sea regions most probably around 1200 B.C. must have been motivated by this general historical phenomenon. They most probably settled in northern Persia and subsequently to south and east of Iranian plateau. We have the authority of Persian poet, Firdausi (935-1020)[4] and also

---

2   The Baloch force formed part of the army of Cambyses.(530-521 B.C).The Shahnama gives the following account of the Baloch fighting against the Median King, Astyages: 'After Gustasham came Ashkash. His army was from the wanderers of Koch and Baloch, intent on war with exalted 'cock-combs' and crest whose back none in the world ever saw, nor was one of their fingers bare of armour. His banner bore the figure of a tiger.

3   Husain Bakhsh Kousar, quoted by Dost Muhammad Dost: The Languages and Races of Afghanistan, Pashtu Academy, Kabul,1975, p.362.

4   Abul Qasim Firdousi completed *Shahnama* on 25th February 1010 A.D. It

strong historical evidence that the Baloch were a political and military force during the time of Cyrus and Cambyses.

However, the Baloch movements from Kerman and Sistan to Makkuran and then Eastern Balochistan was not only the result of the lack of sufficient productive means to meet their demands, or insufficient grazing fields for their flocks, because the area they migrated to was no better in natural resources than the area in which they had been settled for centuries. The main reason was their conflict with rulers and their own internal enmity which resulted in a weakening of their political position. Yet another factor most probably was the Mongolian invasions of Central Asia and the subsequent political anarchy in the whole region.

From the evidence available, it is established that by the beginning of the Christian era, the Baloch was one of the major peoples inhabiting present-day Iranian Balochistan. However, their migration in the semi-deserts and hills of Kerman might have been a survival tactic to avoid the total annihilation by the forces of Sassanid emperor Anushervan (531-578 A.D).

The following account has been given by Firdousi in the Shahnama about Anushervan's war with the Baloch:

> *"The Shah was informed that*
> *The world is wasted by the Baloch,*
> *Till from exceeding slaughter, pillaging, and harrying,*
> *The earth is overwhelmed;*
> *But greater ruin cometh from Gilan,*
> *And curses banish blessing.*
> *Thence the heart of Anushervan, the Shah was sorrowful,*
> *And grief mingled with joy.*
> *He said to the Iranians:*
> *The Alans and Hind were in the terror,*

---

deals with the Persian history of 3874 years. Most of his assertions, however, appear mythical. Given the limitations for an individual at that time, who could face inconveniences in gathering factual evidences apart from legends and events almost defaced throughout centuries, one can presume safely that the *Shahnama* may not be an authentic historical record which could be produced as the only basis to arrive at sound scientific conclusions. Nevertheless, it can hardly be contested that the Baloch played an important part in the political upheavals of Persia during the period mentioned in the *Shahnama*.

Of our scimitars, like silk,
Now our own realm has turned against us,
Shall we hunt lions and forego the sheep?
One said to him: The garden hath no rose without a thorn,
O, King!
So too these marches are ever troublesome and treasure wasting.
As for the Baloch, the Glorious Ardeshir tried with all his
veteran officers,
But all his strategies and artifices,
His labors, arms, feint, and fighting failed.
Though the enterprise succeeded ill,
He cloaked the failures even to himself.
The story of the failures enraged the Shah,
Who went upon his way towards the Baloch.
Now when he drew near those lofty mountains,
He went around them with his retinue,
And all his host encircled them about,
And barred the passage even to wind and ant.
The troops like ants and locusts occupied the mountains and
outskirts to sandy deserts.
A herald went round about the host,
Proclaiming from the caves of the mountains, and plains;
Whenever the Baloch are seeking food,
If they are warriors and carrying arms,
However many or however few,
Let not a single one of them escape.
The troops, aware of the anger of the Shah,
Stopped every outlet with their horse and foot;
Few of the Baloch or none survived.
No women, children warriors, were left:
All of them perished by scimitars,
And all their evil doings had an end,
The world had quiet from their ravagings.
No Baloch, seen or unseen remained,
While on their mountains so it came to pass,
The herd thence forward strayed without a guard,
Alike on waste and lofty mountain tops;
The sheep required no shepherd.
All the folk around thought nothing of past sufferings,
And looked on vale and mountain as their hom,
The wolf's claws grew too short to reach the sheep.

A world without strife with the Baloch had raged:
And filled the cities with distress and anguish;
But by the grace of Anushervan,
The sky had changed its use and favor."

Their migration further east into Makkuran at a later stage was the result of a quarrel between the Kerman ruler and the Baloch Chief. The former demanded forty–four girls one from each Baloch tribe, for his harem. The Baloch dressed up boys in girl's disguise and fearing the wrath of the ruler, migrated from Kerman and took refuge in Makkuran.[5]

The Kurds

The Kurds have been living in the Kurdish region and Zagros area since the Semitic conquest of Assyria. They are said to have created a permanent nuisance for the weak rulers of Assyria by organizing raids on Tigris mainland.[6] In a Sumerian inscription dated 2000 B.C, a country known as Kardala is mentioned; and later the Assyrian King, Tiglath Pileser, (circa745-724 B.C.) appears to have fought a tribe referred to as Kur-ti-e. Xenophon (circa 434-355 B.C.) also speaks of a Kardukai; a mountain–folk who harassed his march towards the sea.[7] Some archaeological evidence tends to show a Kurdish kingdom which flourished in the second millennium B.C on the borders of the Semitic empire in Babylonia. In a later period, the Kurd's cavalry served as the vanguard of Cyrus army in capturing Babylonia in 539 B.C.

The Kurds are from the same origin as that of Baloch. The period of their migration from the Caspian region may be a few centuries earlier than the Baloch who followed at a later period; but instead of going to their people in Zagros mountainous region, outskirts of Mesopotamia, some of them headed towards the east while the majority remained in the western Caspian region. Linguistically and culturally the Baloch and Kurds must have been from the same stock.

---

5   Edward E.Oliwar, Across the Border, Pathan and Baloch, (First published by Chapman and Hall, London 1890) Reprinted by Al. Biruni, Lahore 1977, p.30

6   J.L. Myres, Williama and Norgate, The Dawn of History. London 1918, p.128

7   Hassan Arfa, The Kurds, a Historical and Political Study: Oxford University Press, London, 1968. P 3

Tracing the racial kinship

The term "race" connotes some shared distinctive and inheritable qualities in a people. Psychic, spiritual and physical distinctions are generally regarded as the criteria of race, the formation of which mostly depends on inbreeding and outbreeding of a human group. Migrations and the social-cultural and geographic environment would have a considerable impact on racial characteristics. In an analysis of racial origin, three important factors are to be kept in view: Firstly, similarities of customs and traditions of the ancient peoples living under tribal set-up should be viewed scientifically, and should not be the basis of theories linking the racial origin of a particular people, because cultural homogeneity always exists among all such cultures in a tribal and feudal setting. Secondly, foreign influences on a certain culture throughout a given period form an important factor and must be given serious thought; and thirdly, the geopolitical history of a people should be traced from the earliest times without any prejudice or reservation. Unfortunately, the writers on Baloch history have adopted altogether, a different approach, regardless of most of such important factors and of scientific analysis of the available evidence.

One of the striking facts in the history of Balochistan is that it has been a major gateway for all the ancient conquerors of the Indian subcontinent. It has served at times as a buffer zone between the great powers of the ancient world, Persia, India, and Bactria, and also very often has changed hands among these powers. Apart from this, Arab ascendancy in Central Asia from the 7th century A.D. had its impact. Although the Arab conquests, in the beginning, had least political influences on the Baloch, their inroads to Sistan, Kerman, and Makkuran, though comparatively on a meager scale, must have had certain religious-cultural prevalence on these regions. The Baloch, nevertheless, unlike most people in Central Asia, maintained their cultural identity to a surprisingly great extent; it had, no doubt been influenced by this cultural offensive, but not without invoking deep hatred towards the foreign rule and creating an astounding sense of national pride.

Such historical facts have always been disregarded. On the contrary, there appears to be a psychological compulsion for Baloch writers who are keen to trace its origin to the Semites. Such irresistible approaches are not rare in history. In the early days of Islam in Persia, many Persians changed their names to Arab ones, and fabricated Arab genealogy for themselves to enhance their social status in the eyes of Arab ruler's by claiming kinship with the Arabs. The Persians even claimed that the Prophet's grandson, Husain, married a daughter of Sassanian King, Yazdegerd III (633-651 A.D). After the Muslim breakthrough in Africa, the Berbers, and some other African peoples wished themselves or their rulers to be considered as of Arab origin[8]. In a similar vein, the Baloch were also declared by some of the Baloch writers to have come from Hejaz. In order to flatter the Baloch, the author of *Tohfat el Kiram* traced their origin to Muhammad bin Harun, a descendant of Amir Hamza, Prophet Muhammad's uncle, by a fairy.[9] Similarly, the idea of an esteemed race, for the first time attributed to ancient Hebrews, "a chosen people", was ultimately adopted by many peoples, not always in a religious sense, including ancient Greeks and Romans and by the Aryans after their settlement in the Indian subcontinent. These Baloch writers had perhaps similar considerations in tracing their racial origin, history, and faith.[10] There might still be some cogent reasons for pursuing such historically erroneous presumptions like the Semitic origin of Baloch. This may be due to the desire to find some reactionary consolation by interpreting Baloch history in a particular way, linking it to some distinct people and also digging out sketchy historical evidence of a golden era and glorifying some father figures.[11] This is perhaps the direct result of

8   Reubon Levy, The social Structure of Islam, Cambridge: london,1965, p.60

9   Tohfat el Kiram, quoted by Richard F. Burton, Sind and the Races that inhabit the Valley of Indus (First published London 1851) Reprinted By Oxford University Press, Karachi 1975, pp.237-238.

10   There may be no truth in the assertion that the Baloch were Shia; but the fact that Shiaism prevailed in Iran and was the official sect of powerful empires must have been a good temptation for many to align the Baloch with the Iranian rulers professing that faith. Historically, such misrepresentation is not quite unknown. As mentioned before, the Iranians and some Africans adopted an irrational attitude in boasting their Arab origin; but more recent platitude of Islamic aspects of each and every new scientific discovery linking them very ridiculously to some Muslim scholars of the past, appears to be guided by the same absurd desire. Even the Muslim religious books are being interpreted arbitrarily and often ingenuously to include provisions claimed to have been visualized by their authors or by the prophet to suit the requirements of present era.

11   Nimrod, the Chaldean King, Belus, and Nebuchadrezzar (604-564 B.C)

great upheavals and deep controversies in Baloch society, its economic dependence, and inevitable value re-orientation brought in by foreign domination after many centuries of semi-independence and tribal sway. Some less scrupulous writers visualized every great figure in history as essentially Baloch.[12] Moreover, the oppressor of the Baloch on the Iranian lineage after Anushervan-the late Shah of Iran, Muhammad Reza's boasting of himself as a true representative of the Aryan race must have some apostatizing dislikes on the part of some contemporary Baloch writers to conduct researches with pre-conceived notions, on these lines.

The theory of Baloch being Semites was first propounded by George Rawlinson in 1862 in his three-volume book, The Five Great Monarchies of the Ancient Eastern World. He discussed the possibility that the Baloch might have derived their present name from ancient Babylonian King, Belus, also the name of Great Chaldean god. This has been faithfully followed by some writers. The suggestion by Rawlinson has now least relevance in the face of overwhelming corroborative historical evidence to the contrary. Even if this ill-founded supposition is conceded that Baloch might have come from Babylonia, they are not necessarily Semites. According to the Old Testament, the first Kingdom in these parts was Kushite or Ethiopian. 'And Kush begat Nimrod: he began to be a mighty one in the earth. He was a mighty hunter before the Lord; wherefore it is said, even as Nimrod the mighty hunter before the Lord. And the beginning of his kingdom was Babel and Erech, and Accad and Calneh, in the land of Shinar'.[13] According to this, the early Chaldeans should be Hamites, not Semites-Ethiopians, and Arameans, who should have racial affinities with Abyssinia, southern Arabia, and Gedrosia. The

---

are being glorified as the great ancestors of the Baloch people (see Sardar Khan's History of Baloch Race and Balochistan).

12 Muhammad Husain Unqa's book, Baloch Qoum Ke Doure Qadeen Ki Tharikh (Pakistan Press Quetta, 1974), is perhaps the biggest misinterpretation of history. In the book, almost all the ancient peoples of Asia and the Middle East and their prophets, Kings and warriors were described as Baloch including prophet Abraham with all the traditional Hebrew Kings, the Chaldeans, Babylonians and Assyrians, as also the peoples of Central Asia before and after the Aryan invasion and upto the twentieth century. Many Indian rulers and their prophtet, Buddha also mentioned to be Baloch.

13 Gen. 10:8-10.

Chaldeans, therefore, should have no racial kinship with the peoples who lived in upper Mesopotamia, Syria, Phoenicia, and Palestine.[14]

In Chaldea, to which references are made in connection with being the Baloch original homeland, there inhabited four distinct races, kiprat- arbat, with four distinct languages belonging to four great varieties of human speech: the Hamitic, Semitic, Arian and Turanian.[15] The Biblical assertion has been augmented by the supposition that the language of the original people, called Chaldes, was an Armenian dialect. However, the racial kinship of Babylonians with Assyrians who were Semites may be through some confusion, and established the view that Chaldeans were not necessarily Semites, but most probably Ethiopians and Armenians or at least a mixed race including the Semites.[16] There are faint references in classical literature which refer to Ethiopian, connecting them with the peoples of the Persian Gulf and the Nile Valley; even connecting the Babylonians with the Kushites of Nile. The Greek historians, especially Herodotus *(Circa 484–425 B.C)* has mentioned Ethiopians of Asia whom he very carefully distinguishes from those of Africa. Moreover, the name of Belus has remained attached with Babylonia, a kingdom which is assigned to the people distinctly said to have been Kushite by blood. Inscriptions discovered in Babylonia are supposed to be in the Kushite language. Yet another argument is that the Chaldeans were entirely distinct from the early Babylonians-Armenians, Arabs, Kurds or Sclaves – who came down from the north long after the historical period as the dominant race in the lower Mesopotamia.[17]

The confusion still persists regarding the Asiatic Kush or Ethiopians and their migration to or from Balochistan and India. Their original country was supposed to be either the head of the Persian Gulf or Arabia or south of Egypt from where they might have spread to other regions. It is also believed that these people migrated from the area around the Indus and settled in the territory of the Nile during the reign of Ampelopsis III *(Circa 1410-1375 B.C)*.[18] It may be

---

14   George Rawlinson, *The Five Great Monarchies of Ancient Eastern world*, John Murray, Albemarle Street, London 1862-I, pp 54-55.

15   Ibid. pp, 69-70

16   Ibid.

17   Ibid. p.71.

18   Ibid. pp. 66-67.

mentioned that the territory east of Tigris was known to the Greeks as Cissia or Cossa. The region east of Kerman was some times named Kushan during the Sassanian rule (227-590 A.D).[19]

There are references in early Persian cuneiform inscriptions of Akaufaciya, a people who could be identified with *Kufich, Kufijor Kuj*, also mentioned by Muslim historians including the anonymous author of *Huded al Alam*, a geographic treatise from late 10th century A.D. The author maintains that Kufij lived on the eastern fringe of Kerman and were divided into seven tribes, and who spoke a language of their own.[20] Other Muslim chroniclers, prominent among them al Istakhri and the author of *Burhan-e- Katih*, also localize the *Kuch or Kufij* to Kerman and its eastern regions during the early Islamic period.

Many historians have often associated the "Koch" with Baloch. The Asiatic Ethiopians or Kush of the ancient historians and *Kufij, Kufich, Kuj* of later Arab and Persian chroniclers are one and the same people. It is possible that after the Baloch hegemony in these areas, Koch or Kuch many have lost their separate identity and merged with the newcomers, and for quite some time to come referred with the new people as 'Koch o Baloch', the remnants of this people are found in the entire region. The classical literature mentions Asiatic Ethiopians as dark-colored with straight and sometimes crispy hairs.[21] This description fits many people in the subcontinent and Balochistan. As regards their relations with the Baloch, the description could come true to indigenous but now 'Balochised' inhabitants of southern Balochistan.

Mesopotamia and its adjoining regions from time immemorial were the most fertile lands and the seat of a great civilization which attracted other peoples to these areas. There are virtually very few instances in history that there had been any migrations on a large scale from Mesopotamia or Chaldea to the east. If the Baloch were Semites inhabiting Mesopotamia or Chaldea, there must have been some vestige of these people in the Middle East. There is hardly any trace of them in the remote ages in those areas, save the Kurds who came from the Caspian region towards the west a few centuries earlier than the Baloch. Moreover, a civilized people like the Chaldeans could

---

19   Ibid, pp. 62-63.

20   Hudud Al Alam, quoted by yu. v. Gankovsky. op. *Cit*, p 34.

21   Rawlinson, Op. Cit, p.66.

not reverse to nomadic life and tribalism soon after their migration from their original country.

The discussion cannot reach any logical conclusion until we have a detailed account of the Semites as well as the other main racial group, the Aryans. We could attempt to establish some relationship if any, of the Baloch with either of that racial group after we have an unprejudiced description of those people and their origin.

The adjective, 'Semite', is an eighteenth-century term coined by a German historian, Schlozer, in 1781 to denote a group of closely related languages. The Semite referred subsequently to peoples who might have spoken those languages. They are classified as the Semites, not because they possessed any unique physiological features in common but chiefly because they all appear to have migrated from Central Arabian Peninsula. The Semites have supposed to have descended from the biblical character of Shem, the eldest son of Noah. They are represented mainly by the Jews[22] and the Arabs, and by ancient Babylonians, Assyrians, Amorites, Armenians, Canaanites, and the Phoenicians. Among the Semitic languages, Arabic, Ethiopic, and Hebrew are still spoken. Most of the languages of the group, Akkadian and Canaanite, are dead, while Aramaic survived in a much-altered form.

The Semitic migrations took place mostly in three phases: Akkadians in Mesopotamia during 4th millennium B.C; Western Semites (Cananeo- Phoenicians and Amorites) in Mesopotamia and Syriac-Palestine during the third and second millennium B.C; the Armenians to the fertile crescent in the 12th century B.C, and Nabalaeans (Nabataeans) and other Arabs from the second century B.C to the advent of Islam.[23]

The first Semitic migration took place about 3500 B.C. from Arabian Peninsula, along the west coast of Arabia, through Hejaz and Sinai into Egypt where the Semites were mixed up with Hamites

---

22 Jewish people first moved into Canaan most probably from Ur under the leaderdship of Abraham, the Hebrew, and settled in the vicinity of Habron. The second wave of Jews settled around Schem under the leadership of Jacob, the Israel, the eponymous ancestor of the Israelites. The third wave of them entered Canaan from the east and south around the end of the 13th and the beginning of the 14th century B.C.

23 George Roux, *Ancient Iraq*, George Allen & Unwin, London, 1964 pp.124-125

to produce the Egyptian civilization. Another migration struck up the eastern shores of Arabia and settled in Tigris- Euphrates valley where they United with the non-Semites, the Sumerians to produce the Babylonians and like their counterpart in Egypt adapt local culture and methods to their needs. A thousand years later, a further mixed population in Syria and Palestine created the Amorites and Phoenicians; and a thousand years after that, between 1500 and 1200 B.C. the nomadic Hebrews arrived in Palestine and later on established the world's first monotheistic faith.

The Semites have further been divided into various groups; as also Semitic languages. The north-central Semitic group includes the Canaanite Ugaritic and Amorite languages of the ancient stage which were spoken in Palestine. Phoenician was spoken in Syria and Mesopotamia from the third to second millennium B.C. The middle stage belongs also to Phoenician and Punic, Hebrew and Old Aramaic. Hebrew was spoken in Palestine from 13th century B.C. The southern central Semitic group of languages included Arabic of ancient and Middle stage and Akkadian beginning from 3200 B.C.

Like the Semites, the Aryans, too, who are presumed to be a race because of the group of languages known as the Indo-European, must have had a common origin. It is, like the Semite, a linguistic term; and it would be inaccurate to refer to it as a people whose ethnic identity is least known on the basis of historical evidence so far available.

The Aryan migration has been steady and taken place in successive waves. The first to arrive on the Iranian Plateau, around the middle of the second millennium, is termed Indo-Iranians. They moved from the region of the Oxus and Jaxartes rivers. The Iranians came around 900 BC: they appear to have lived in settled communities and spoken an Indo-European tongue. They most probably supplemented the earlier immigrants.

The earliest migration of the Indo-European peoples had been towards the middle of the second millennium B.C. when the Achaeans entered Greece, and the Aryans spread into Italy and Asia Minor. In the course of their migration, the Indo-Europeans apparently split into two main groups: one the Western branch, rounded the Black Sea, crossed into Balkans and the Bosporus, penetrated into Asia Minor, and later on formed a Hittite Confederation. They also appeared in Syria and Egypt. Another, the Eastern branch, moved eastwards and rounded the Caspian Sea. One group among them crossed the

Caucasus and pushed as far as the great bend of the Euphrates where they settled among the indigenous Hurrians and later on formed the Kingdom of Mitanni in 1450 B.C. They established their suzerainty over northern Mesopotamia and Zagros. Then the bulk of the Aryans pressed eastwards, crossed the Oxus and entered Bactrian plains. They scaled the passes of the Hindu Kush along the Panjsher and Kabul rivers. Quite a few tribes might have thrust towards the West [24] and probably southwest to the present Afghan, Pakistani and Iranian parts of Balochistan. The Aryan migration to the Iranian plateau from the Caspian Sea region early in the first millennium B.C seems to have been the second Aryan eruption. A group of tribes named "the Iranian" came to the Iranian plateau about 900 B.C. The whole region was originally called Iran, the land of the Aryans, after the Aryan tribes who settled in the region. Persia denotes the area in south-west Iran near the Persian Gulf, around the historic cities of Pasargadae and Persepolis, also known as Persia by the Greeks and Fars by the Arabs. Iran became a superpower during Achaemenian rule; however, the present country of Iran was originally called Persia until 1935 when Iran was officially adopted as the name of Persia by Shah Reza Khan Pahlavi reflecting pride in the Aryan or Achaemenian past.

It is fairly evident from cuneiform sources that the Medes and the Persian and other Iranian peoples were moving into Western Iran from the east. They must have followed routes along the south of Elburz mountains; and as they entered the Zagros, spread out to the northwest and southwest following the natural topography of the mountains.

It is, however, not clear that the Aryans spoke one language. Like the peoples themselves, the language must invariably be numerous. But the dialects perhaps one way or the other gave way to one major speech, the Sanskrit. The Aryan literature was quite elaborate, and its unbroken traditions are the oldest in the world. The Rig Vedic hymns (1500-1000 B.C) which still form the core of Hindu sacred literature were transmitted orally for centuries before they were written down in Sanskrit. Another main language which flourished as a result of this vast population movement is Avesta and its sub-branches. The Indo-Aryan and the Iranian languages together constitute the Indo-Iranian

---

24 R. Ghirshman, Iran, from Earliest Times to the Islamic Conquest, Penguin Books, London, 1978, p 63.

family of languages. The Indo-Aryan languages are mostly spoken in the subcontinent and Himalayan regions.

The discussion regarding the Baloch racial origin cannot be confined to the Aryan or Semitic groups. Attention should also be focused on another migration of a central Asian origin which settled at Susa around the third millennium B.C. These peoples are known as Elamites. They came from either the Oxus and Jaxartes or further afield towards the heart of Asia. Although little is known about these peoples, it appears that the Elamites, Kassites, the Lullabi and Guti belonged to the same racial group and spoke related languages.[25]

By the third quarter of the third millennium B.C, the Elamites formed a dynasty which ruled over a wide area including some important parts of the Gulf and Bushire region of present-day Iran. The Elamites soon afterward engaged in a conflict with the Semitic empire of Babylonia during the reign of Sargon (2371-2316 B.C) with the result that the Elamites were completely annihilated and Susa was captured and annexed by Sargon dynasty (2371-2230 B.C).

From the Sargon conquests till the second millennium B.C. a period of nearly a thousand years, little is known about the Elamites. In the second millennium B.C, they formed a dynasty in Elam whose kings styled themselves as 'divine messengers father and King' of Anzan and Susa. This kingdom also diminished after its conflict with the powerful Babylonian King, Hammurabi (1792-1750 B.C).

It may be mentioned that before the Elamite settlements, Susa was the seat of an earlier civilization. It had its own script known as 'proto- Elamite'. The people had constant contacts with the Sumero-Semitic population of the western plains. The Elamites themselves were largely influenced by the Sumerian culture. This is confirmed by the Sumerian script found in Susa.[26]

What the Elamite settlements in Susa signify in the context of the Baloch racial origin is yet to be established, but we cannot rule out the remote possibility that the Baloch may belong to the Elamites and might have migrated much earlier than the Aryans. As regards Kurds, they migrated in the same period or a little earlier and lived side by side with the Elamites.

---

25 .Ibid. p 50.

26 . Ibid, p.52.

Racial origin: main factors

While determining the racial kinship of a people, an objective study on scientific lines is required of the physical traits or biological growth; languages, their structure and possible changes; folklore and literature; religion and mythologies; social and political institutions and cultural affinity with other peoples, keeping in view the general characteristics of all tribal and feudal societies of a given period in the past. Several other points including geography and environmental changes have also to be taken into account. While judging the racial kinship, the inseparable elements of language and culture, save certain genuine exceptions, must always be kept in view. Culture is always depicted through language which is one of the guiding factors in classifying the human group. However, an unscientific approach has been followed by writers on this aspect of Baloch history. A judicious and scientific study of Balochi language and culture, religion and mythologies which are the pre-requisites, were never attempted; nor the Baloch political and socio-economic institutions were analyzed to find out any similarities or dissimilarities with any culture and people.

Language and literature

The theory linking the Balochi Language with Semitic, which is not based on sound historical evidence, was inappropriately followed by some writers. It has been wrongly presumed that Balochi has drawn words from the same sources as Arabic, particularly from Chaldean branch of the Semitic languages. Nevertheless, certain Semitic influences on Balochi may have come through Aramaic, a Semitic tongue, which was the official language of the Persian Empire during the Achaemenid (546-330 B.C) rule. The language did not fall in use even much after the Achaemenid Empire disintegrated. The language had an easy script and was taken over from the Assyrians.[27] There are also evidences that the Aramaic alphabet was used for writing old Persian.[28] But linking Balochi with any Semitic language is altogether based on wrong premises. The premise had been made without

---

27 John Bowle, A New Outline of World History: From the Origin to Eighteenth Century, George. Allen & Unwin, London 1962, p.72.

28 R. Ghirshman, Op. Cit, p.164.

considering many ingredients of the linguistic record, analyzing the sounds, vocabulary, grammatical structure, and moreover, the slow process of language change throughout history. The most appropriate approach adopted should have been a scientific comparison of the characteristics of two languages or group of languages whose cognation is asserted, in order to arrive at some formulations. The most ancient vocabulary, as well as the word elements used to express grammatical relations, are the main criteria for classifying language groups. A few common words cannot establish such relations which could be deduced as a result of minute research and sound proofs of phonological structure and inflectional forms. It is also difficult to ascertain precisely from linguistic evidence alone the date at which any group of language must have begun diverging.

Moreover, the relationship of various language groups or a particular language cannot be established without following the fundamental course of linguistic change. Factors such as population movement and domination of one people by another are major determinants in classifying any language or group of languages. Isolated loan-words [29] and even some phonological similarity cannot be cited as scientific proofs of any language kinship. Loan-words creep into the language as a result of contact with other languages or of technological and scientific changes. This is a historical process, and every language must experience such occurrences. For instance, in the areas adjoining the Pakistani provinces of Sindh and Punjab, Balochi has many words derived from Sindhi and Punjabi. Similarly, as Urdu is being introduced as Lingua Franca and has been given the status of the national language of Pakistan, many words of Urdu have crept not only into Balochi but also into other languages of Pakistan. Balochi spoken in Iran and Afghanistan has many words from Persian and Pashtu, the official languages of those countries respectively. Therefore, any opinion based on a few loanwords about language

---

29 Balochi has quite a few loan-words from Turkish and Arabic. Turkish words might have come mostly through Persian. The Arabic words are the result of religious and political hegemony of the Arabs in Balochistan since 7th century A.D. It is absolutely untenable to assert that Balochi has drawn words from the same sources as Arabic. Muhammad Sardar Khan Baloch (See, A Literary History of the Balochis, I, p. 4) has maintained that Balochi drew word from the sources as Chaldean. His assertion is based apparently on a few loan-words in Balochi.

kinship is superfluous. Moreover, little evidence is available to find the exact era at which any ancient language was spoken in a certain area, nor can we determine the nature of possible changes in the vocabulary and the basic structure of any distant tongue, apart from certain rare exceptions. This handicap should by no means provide a pretext for conjectural assertions in language relationship.

The process of linguistic change makes it very difficult, however, to establish the language kinship or the fact that any existing speech really represents the original or any ancient tongue except that of a possible affiliation which may be inferred only through an objective study of existing differences or similarities of present dialects which are no less than 2700. Although the races cannot be determined on the basis of language alone, it is perhaps the strongest element in such a study. In any ultimate analysis of racial affinity, the language is the first and foremost factor. It is the most important instrument of socialization in all human cultures. Language passes its myths, laws, customs, and beliefs to the next generation. It is only through language that one could appreciate the essence of any social structure. Culture and language go together. If language is transmitted as a part of the culture, it is no less true that culture is transmitted through language. Therefore, the language and literature of a particular people furnish a lot of facts regarding the general character of those people. For instance, the heroic verses and prose tales in Balochi literature and its magical and mystery cults show that it is a race of unsettled warriors throughout centuries. This is only one aspect any language could represent the race.

Many people do not speak the same language but are still regarded as one race. The Baloch tribes and Jewish people do not speak one language; so also many other people who have been classified into one or other racial group but speak different tongues. The Ugandan tribe, Amba, speak two mutually unintelligible languages but they are considered one people. Our immediate neighbors, the Pakhtuns, speak different tongues. Sadozai and Mahmadzai among them do not speak Pashtu, so also a great majority of them living in Kabul and areas adjacent to Iran, but they constitute one people, the Pakhtuns.

The proposition that the Baloch either lost their Semitic tongue and substituted it with an Aryan dialect, or the language itself has been so influenced by the Aryan dialect that it lost its Semitic character[30] is totally untenable. Balochi has least influences whatsoever of any Semitic language except for a few Arabic words which have come after 7th century A.D. through political and religious hegemony of the Arabs in Iran and Central Asia.

Linguistically, Balochi is an Aryan language closely related to Kurdish, which must have been a branch of the ancient mother tongue of those two peoples. It is among the Iranian branch of Indo-Iranian languages; the other members of this included Farsi, Pushto, Kurdi, Kurmani, Gilaki, Mazanderani, Talyshi, Ossetic, etc. There are, however, loan-words in Balochi from other Indo-European languages.[31]These inflections are not of a fundamental nature and could not have changed its basic character. Balochi appears to be more archaic than Persian. It has admirably resisted the phonetic changes throughout centuries which is amply evident from the pure Balochi words preserved mainly in Balochi heroic poems and ballads.[32] Balochi is, however, far from being homogeneous. Baloch living in Pakistani provinces of Sindh and Punjab speak a dialect greatly influenced by Punjabi and Sindhi. Balochi spoke in Chagai and Afghani Balochistan, Makkuran, Kerman, and Sistan have their dialectical variations, influenced by the neighboring languages. But with all its dialectical heterogeneity it has a separate character of its own nevertheless closely linked with Sanskrit[33] and the old Persian.

---

30 Mir Khuda Bakhsh Mari, Searchlights on Baloches and Balaochistan, Royal Book Company, Karachi 1974, p. 31.

31 Muhammad Abdur Rehman Barker and Mir Aqil Khan Mengal, A course in Balochi, Institution of Islamic Studies, Megill University, Montreal, Canada 1969 I, p xxIII.

32 A.J. Arberry(ed), The legacy of Persia, Oxford, London 1953, pp. 194-195.

33 Balochi is closely linked with Sanskrit. Most of the pure Balochi words were generally used in Sanskrit with almost the same meanings. However, while tracing the language kinship instead of comparing mere words the best criteria should be comparing words and phrases which have deep cultural or religious touch or which may indicate that such relations really existed between the two languages. The following have been chosen for their importance vis-a-vis the relationship of Balochi with Sanskrit:

Sanskrit	English meaning	Balochi
man	me	man
tuvam	thou	thou

It resembles many other Iranian languages in showing a nearer

kuda	when	kadi
kas	who	kas
asti	is	asth
asha	this	esh
bhuta	been	butha
na	not	na
janati	he knows	zaanthe
pitar	father	peth
ma	mother	maath
bhrater	brother	braath
duhitar	daughter	duhthar
asvas	horse	asp
mrga	bird	murg
ushtar	camel	ushther
mesh	sheep	meish
pad	foot	paad
leb	lip	lunt, lab
danth	tooth	danthaan
pantha	journey	pand
dirghas	long	draaj
navas	new	nok
bandh	bind	band
han	strike	jan
nar-ay	go out	narray
parmana	command	parmaan
zaath	caste	zaath
badan	body	badan
shap	night	shap
jingal	jingal	dumbaal
sati	sari	sari
dad	hard	dadd
kula	family, home	kull/kahol
Sur	move or moving	sur
karpas	cotton	karpaas

relationship to ancient Avesta than to the old Persian, the Court language of the Achaemenids, from which modern Persian is distinctly descended.[34]

The intimate ties between the language of the Avesta, especially in its earliest form recorded in the Gathas, and the language of the Vedic hymns, furnish ample evidence that ancient Iranian dialects

godam	grain, wheat	gandeem
kumb	water container	kumb
ap	water	aap
zik	ghee or wine container	zikk
laja	shyness, modesty, honour	lajj
		(cont. over leep)
baraze	characteriszaion of fire, blaze	braanz
angar/angaar	fire	angar,
pul/bul	to snatch or draw	pul
lunt	loot	lutt
mareg	mark, visible impression, feeling	maarag
sthga	cheat, thug	tagg
Band	embankment, bund	band
Nekh	nail	naakun
Moshk	rat	mushk
Kag	crow	guraag, kalaag
Ekas	one	yak
Duva	two	do
Traya	three	say
Catavaras	four	chaar
Panca	five	panch
Sat	six	shash
Sapta	seven	hapth
Asta	eight	hashth
Nava	nine	noh
Davas	ten	dah
Satam	hundred	sad

34 George Abrahm, lingulstic Survey of India, Calcutta, 1921, p.33

were widely spoken among the peoples living in Gedrosia,[35] southern slopes of Hindu Kush, northern parts of Bactria and Aria. Their ties seem to date from the beginning of first millennium B.C and verify the close contact of the Aryans with the speakers of the Avesta. The most probable zone of this contact being area adjacent to the basin of the Helmand River.[36]

Balochi's affinity with Persian is understandable because of the close links of the two people for centuries. Persian has been the official language of powerful empires. It was but natural that Balochi should have been influenced by that language. It originated neither from Parthian nor Middle Persian. It may, however, have shared some features with both languages as of Median speech[37].

Unlike Sanskrit, the language of the Aryan, Balochi has no written record. The poetry which can be traced from fifteenth century A.D. is found in a highly developed form. It leaves little doubt that such a developed shape in literature must have been the result of centuries of development, but little traces of its development are available, and therefore, least could be deduced without authentic evidence.

The folk literature, oral in nature, which includes folk tales and lore, provides support for the institutions and behavior patterns of a deep-rooted culture. Folk stories though generally considered as pure fiction have great appeal to the people of all ages in the community who generally never challenge the essence of all that is narrated. The folklore, especially the proverbs and fables, serve to instruct and remind the members of the society of a wise code of conduct and social behavior.

Cultural and religious traditions

Culture is the integrated whole of learned behavior traits and characteristics of the member of a given society. It constitutes a people's lifestyle, its entire activity. The general morale of a people

---

35 Yu, V Gankovsky, Op. Cit, p 62.

36 Ibid.

37 George Abrahm, lingulstic Survey of India, Calcutta, 1921 p.33
    Yu, V Gankovsky, Op. Cit, p 62.

which is a cultural innovation has also its role in establishing the cultural affinity or diversity of a given people. Culture is also determined by the genetic make –up of its founders. The second most important criterion which is inseparably linked with language is the culture which cannot be neglected while classifying or establishing racial kinship of various peoples. It reflects not only the economic life of a people but has a long range of socio-political and religious aspects. Most people removed from their ancestral culture have maintained cultural affinity with their people.

All socio-cultural systems exist in a natural habitat where environmental changes have a greater impact. It is asserted that even styles of myths and tales are reshaped by topography and climate. The environment encourages or even prohibits certain cultural traits. Notwithstanding, it may be maintained that the environment as an essential factor, may not determine the culture altogether.

Religion and mythology are also the basic constituents of human culture. They occur in the history of all human traditions. Every culture has developed a stock of myths which always indicate the self-image of a people. Although myths are now dismissed as a senseless distortion of events, or some fantastic occurrences or part of dead religions or mere personification of some philosophical or abstract idea[38], it has undoubtedly a great relevance and rationale which certainly helps in analyzing the general approaches of a people or groups of people. It still largely represents the genius of a people, their literature and folk. History itself mostly grew out of mythology, which gives most curious answers to complex questions which the primitive mind was unable to explain. While probing the racial kinship of a particular people, its myths which are found in its literature must invariably be taken into account. Myths have helped the modern man to understand the great ancient religions of Greeks and Hindus by providing a sound religious background.

Apart from being something essential in all primitive peoples, its relative prosperity, cultural and political outlook, and religious beliefs should lead to conclusions about history. The ancient saint- heroes of Greek religion, for example, ultimately led to the idea that the mighty deads continued to live even after their death, as strong spiritual powers. Beliefs in kings having super-natural powers have led to many

---

38 Bergen Evan, Dictionary of Mythology, Dell Publishing Company, New York 1972 p,5.

33

other social beliefs, permanent institutions, and powerful cultural taboos. Historical heroes acquire supernatural attributes. They became the symbols and standard bearers of national goals and objectives. Therefore, a study of religious traditions could help in arriving at conclusions regarding racial kinship.

Physical traits

Studies on various stages and aspects of human biological growth include studies on stature, head shape or cephalic index, the size, and structure of the brain, eye color, skin color, the texture of hair, the epicanthic fold, constitutional structure of the body, body odor and blood groups. However, in modern times, it has become difficult to arrive at some sound conclusions regarding race homogeneity on the theories based on classical comparison of races on the basis of merely physical observation and measurement or upon differences or similarities in genetics or both. A great many factors are to be considered in establishing racial affiliation. Nevertheless, if we follow the classical theory of physical observation and measurement for race analysis, with the skull/face measurements of some Central Asian and Semitic races, conducted by physical anthropologists, it is fully established that the Baloch skull indexes and structure belong to Brachycephalic Iranians and not related to Dilochocephalic Semites.[39]

The race formation depends largely upon inbreeding or outbreeding which is mostly determined by geographical isolation and change. It also depends upon the adaptation of the unstable human organism to the demand of the physical and cultural environments. The human organism has shown itself to be capable of adapting physical changes to varied climatic conditions, diets, and requirements of cultural adjustment.

The human races[40] always drift genetically. They are in a continual state of transformation. Numerous migrations and cultural mingling of

---

39 Long Worth Dames, The Ethnography and Historical Sketch of the Baloch Race, Trans: Gul Khan Naseer Koch o Baloch, Balochi Publications Karachi, 1969, pp 116-117.

40 The term race must not be confused with the term nation which has only certain characteristics in common, while race has some collective heritable physical and cultural traits. Distinctly manifest psychic and spiritual

various people have throughout centuries served as a dynamic process of change in the human biological history. Besides, the large migration of peoples, explorers, military men, and others contributed their genes to the populations they visited. Peoples inhabiting the plains of north India, Sindh, and Punjab for instance, are of mixed origin as a result of centuries of conquests and raids by outside forces who have brought in the new genes to their captives and war brides. These factors have made it difficult to assert the ethnic purity of any people beyond certain exceptions.

The human population has been arbitrarily divided into many groups: Mongoloid, Caucasoid, Negroid, with numerous divisions or sub-races. Such divisions are mostly based on skin color, i.e. black-man, white- man, yellow-man, and red-man. Races are constituted hypothetically to justify the distribution of genetic characteristics. Races have also been inferred from archaeological discoveries. Similarly, the term 'Semite' was conceived more appropriately as an extension of Biblical thinking.

The Baloch Aryan Origin

The Baloch culture which should be the main criteria in closely examining not only its character but also the lost relationship of its language and people with other groups has its roots in socio-political and religious systems inherited from its Aryan ancestors. Throughout history, the Baloch like most other peoples had great pressure; political, social, economic and military, but had resisted such pressures and their linguistic and cultural transformation had been surprisingly very slow and without any mark or drastic impact on their general cultural outlook.

Like the Aryans, the Baloch society was based on tribalism and had a clan system which is still intact. The tribal Chief was revered. He enjoyed great prestige. He had a pivotal position in all walks of tribal life. The Aryan political, social and economic system was based on primitive tribalism. The tribes were organized as patriarchal groups. The Chief enjoyed tremendous powers. There is no trace of any permanent legal institutions at early ages. However, the *Sardar*, with the help of section heads decided the disputes. Disputes regarding

---

characteristics are also considered the main attributes of a race.

land or inheritance appear to be rare. Polygamy was unknown, and polyandry is mentioned in later writing.[41] Vedic literature refers to the re-marriage of an Aryan widow, generally with the husband's brother.

There are least historical evidence to indicate whether the Aryans imposed the caste system in India or the system existed before their arrival. However, the proud Aryans maintained their distinction and were reluctant to mix up with the natives for fear of losing their identity. The natives were darker in color, called Dasas. They were of the 'Snub-nose' and 'Strange speech' in all probability of the early Dravidians. The Sanskrit word for the cast, Varna, literally means color in Vedic times. The Aryans were *dwija* which means a twice-born caste, the first being physical birth and the second, the initiation into caste status.[42] The Baloch word 'waja' etymologically is 'dwija' in Sanskrit, connoting a superior status and place of respect.[43]

The early Aryans were polytheists. Their mode of worship was based mostly on sacrifices. Their main concern was nature. This can be deduced from the fact that most of the Vedic gods were forces of nature, like the sun, the moon, fire, storm and so on. The fundamental religious ideas were those of primitive animism where the force which could not be controlled or understood was invested with divinity and personified as male or female gods.

Discussing the Indian mythologies, their present form came down from the ancient times and must be the result of the amalgamation of the Aryan and non-Aryan Indus Valley peoples' mythologies. Secondly, the Aryan contact with other groups of the same people who had been settled in Western Iran close to the Middle East may not have been broken; and some kind of influence from the Middle Eastern mythologies through the Aryan peoples in constant move may have been felt on the Indian frontiers. The Aryan contact with Central and West Asia after their settlement in the Indian subcontinent is apparent from many pieces of evidence and also from the close kinship between Sanskrit and the earliest surviving Iranian languages.

---

41 Romila Thaper, *A History of India*, I Penguin Books, London, 1977, P 44.

42 Ibid. P 38.

43 In Balochi *waja* means noble, respected, and has the same etymological origin as that of Sanskrit, *dwija*. It is however not clear whether the earlier Baloch connoted the word in the same philosophical sense as *dwija* or not.

Baloch mythologies have a great resemblance with those of the Aryans. The Baloch myth of a naked or semi-naked woman to be sent to the cattle in the night to save them from the enterostomia is no doubt of Aryan origin. Similarly, to cause rain it was believed that a naked woman should plow the parched fields. This is an Indian myth still believed by some Indian peoples. On the 27th of August 1979, in the Indian State of Uttar Pradesh, naked women plowed parched fields at night to propitiate the rain god. The popular belief was that the god would appear only when women work in the field at night completely undressed.[44] The Baloch did not believe in such myths. However, *Kaalaan Kambaru*, that is painting a boy to have a ugly look, carrying him to every house, repeating *kaalaan Kambaru*, getting some articles from each house to be finally cooked in an isolated place; or the girls *shishalaan shaalu thrampoke aap de* exercises are clearly of the Aryan origin and widely practiced among the Baloch.

There are wide ranges of mythological beliefs and cultural practices common among the various Aryan groups and the Baloch. In the Vedic culture, it appears that the newly married couple would not have intercourse on the first night of the marriage because they thought it might displease the gods. This was in vogue till recently among the Baloch. They considered it improper to cohabit with the bride on the first night. While reaping the wheat crops, the Baloch generally left a small portion of it unreaped, devoting it to gods and praying for a bumper crop at the next season. In a later period in history, the practice continued without any religious touch; and the unreaped crops were apportioned for many servile dependents; the original practice had its genesis in the Aryan customs. The Baloch men wearing '*durr*' earring, which is an Aryan practice.

The Baloch associated certain species of animals with sorcerers and witches. They believed that an animal which is overpowered or whose soul is bound up to that of the sorcerer may be ordered to serve his evil master. The *Jaathu (the sorcerer)* can also assume the form of that animal. Although this is a universal phenomenon, the Aryan touch in it is still preserved and believed. The Baloch thought that the witches or *Jaathu* always rode the hyena. The *Kaheeri*, the legendary saints, first mentioned in Baloch ballads of the 15th century, are said to have ridden the tree, *Kaheer* {prosodies spicier}, therefore

---

44 Balochistan Times, Quetta, 29 August 1979.

they are called Kaheeri. Animals and plants have played important roles in many cultures. The Baloch considered the fox as clever and mischievous while owl as ominously evil.

The Aryans like most other ancient peoples believed in the existence of marvelous creatures. We find a lot of such creatures in Balochi folk-tales. Circumstantial meeting of these amorphous beings with humans was believed to result in pleasant omens or distressing fortunes. In some stories such creatures marry and consort with human beings. They reward human services and punish misdeeds.

The verbal element is considered a fundamental constituent of magical power. While narrating folk stories or legends, the storyteller most often interrupted their narration by uttering meaningless words and phrases which apart from inciting inattentive listeners must have invariably been aimed to have some magical effect. If anybody from among the listeners would say, 'ay walla' the storyteller stopped the narrative and uttered some meaningless words like the following: *Kuchk Majole, danthaan suhre, ushthiri neshe jangala kapthag: chisthaan chisthaan panaahe regithaan.* Almost all the storytellers used similar words with slight variations or additions of their own. This is of Aryan origin.

Among the early Aryans, it appears that there were neither any rules for worship nor the presence of any priest during ceremonies was essential. The Baloch preserved this approach for centuries but subsequently while assimilating beliefs of other peoples, ritualistic ceremonies were more formalized. Ancestor-worship of the Aryans is the result of later alien influence and does not appear to be a purely Aryan practice. Offerings made to the ancestors in the later Vedic period was the result of the mingling of various races. It is evident from *Puranas* and *Mahabharata* that ancestor- worship must be a later innovation.

The Balochi epics knit together a great mass of ancient traditions, customs, legends, prudential maxims, and spiritual discourses. There are great reminiscences to the epics of Ramayana and Mahabharata or with Homeric Greek epics, with Balochi war songs, which mostly depict a pastoral and nomadic way of living. The Indian sacred books or the Greek Homeric poems, the *Iliad* and the *Odyssey*, provide apparently a rational background for many myths, social practices and traditional outlook in a customary way. The Balochi epics while describing the heroes and their achievements contain the very essence of Baloch society and system. If properly analyzed, the fundamental pattern appears to be the same with Indian epics. Balochi ballads of the earliest period date back only to the fifteenth century in their present form, while the Indian epics were composed in nearly 1000 B.C. What is surprising is that minus the stories of gods and goddesses, both epics have the same lucidity, forceful expression, and style.

The Aryan touch in music has not been lost until today. Indian music developed as a beautiful melange of Aryan and Indian music, while Baloch classical pattern appears to be preserved with very few changes and has a great resemblance to Indian Raags. Balochi raga *bashkard* which is an extension of *Kurdi* raga is very close in its structural form to Hindi *Raag Darbari*. Raags, classified as Balochi, including *meedi*, have a similar relationship in form and forcefulness with various Hindi raags. Similarly, Balochi *zaheerag* is undoubtedly of Aryan origin in its essence, meaning, and structure. Some musical instruments, like *nal-sur* and *thamburag*, are undisputedly Central Asian instruments still preserved among the Baloch.

The Baloch is a proud people with a great sense of self- esteem. A Baloch usually swore by his own head or by the head of his father. Among the Baloch, the caste system had not that much strictness as created and maintained by other Aryan groups who settled in the subcontinent where the caste system had ultimate religious sanctions. Most probably, it was on the philosophical basis that most Indian people believed that all living being were divided into *genera* or classes, and each of which was thought to possess a definite coded substance. Like many other Central Asiatic peoples where belonging to a particular caste was considered a matter of perfection, both individually and collectively, the Baloch, however, had a different system closely akin to a somewhat Indianized form of Aryan social structure i.e. Tribal differentiation. The non-Baloch tribes and the natives were never accorded equal status in the tribal set-up. Most of such tribes though '*Balochized*' after centuries of co-existence are to some extent, still regarded racially inferior.

One of the deep-rooted cultural characterizations of the Aryan, the indissolubility of the *Kula,* family, has its reminiscence among the Baloch. Conceptually, the Baloch *Kahol* (the family), has provided not only the psychological bond cementing the unity of the family and common traditions which were handed down from father to son, but also fostered a collective consciousness among the family and ultimately the entire people were tied up in common descent. Like the Aryans, the Baloch *kahol* was the elementary cell of the culture, providing the norms of conduct, and training its members from birth to death on all aspects of the Baloch traditional values. It inspired the love and pride of parentage. It was the perennial source of stability, vitality, and continuity of the Baloch culture. In its essence, the Baloch family is undoubtedly the prototype of the *Kula* of the Aryans.

The Aryan administrative system, though rudimentary at the beginning, accorded the tribal chief, afterward the King, a pivotal position. The tribal confederacy or kingdom, *Rashtra*, contained tribes (*Jana*), tribal units (*Vish*), and villages (*Grama*). The nucleus was the family (*Kula*), with the eldest male member as its head (*kulapa*). The chief was assisted by the tribal units and the villages' Headmen.[45] This is almost the same pattern the Baloch still have maintained with slight modification, keeping in view the changing circumstance and social advancement. The Aryan *sabha and semiti*, the tribal assemblies, have their reminiscences among the Baloch. The *sabha* may have been a council of tribal elders deciding important matters, whereas the *semiti* may have been a general assembly of the entire tribe convened only in cases of grave emergency.[46] In the Baloch tribal set-up, these assemblies were, however, less frequent.

Like the Aryans, the educational and entertainment center of the Baloch was the house of the Chief or elder where history, legends, ballads, and dramas were told and sung. Lyrics and tales of romance were recited. The posing of riddles was also common. In a later stage, perhaps due to the different conditions there were permanent storytellers or bards. This became a sort of institution and the bards did invariably add or curtail some of the legendary folks to suit the changing mythological, religious and social requirements. While their Aryan ancestors acquired writing when they came into contact with civilization, the Baloch most probably were not accustomed to writing until recent epochs. Memories of the bards were the only living literature passing from generation to generation. They have their legendary history, folk and poetry crystallized in bardic recitations, epics, and war ballads.

---

45 Romila Thapar, Op. Cit, p.38.

46 Ibid. p.37.

The Baloch culture, its religion, mythologies, and language have no similarity or resemblance with the Semites. If there is any minor similarity, it should be viewed from a wider perspective of general external influences, mainly Mesopotamian and Assyrian. In the Baloch folk stories, characters of superhuman figures, part human and part bull or animal, is clearly of Middle Eastern origin which has come through a Sumerian and Assyrian form. Gilgamesh-like heroes who see everything anywhere in the Baloch stories with godly qualifications have Babylonian mythological resemblances with slightly different versions according to local surroundings.

Balochistan has been an important strategic area throughout recorded history. It had provided a channel of communication between Persia and the subcontinent and served as a trade link between the Middle East, Iran, and the Central Asian countries. The passage that connected India with the Middle East and Central Asia passed through Afghanistan and Balochistan, which has from time immemorial served as a promising trade track. Evidence point to the existence of the famous Tehran Mashad route connecting Bactria with Mesopotamia. A southern route through Yezd, Kerman, and Makkuran; linking Mesopotamia, Iran, and Bactria was also in operation.[47] There is literary and archaeological evidence of trade between the Indus civilization and Mesopotamia even before the Aryan invasion. The Harapan seals were used to seal the bundles of merchandise, as clay seals at Ur and other Mesopotamian cities. The discovery of a Persian type of seal at Lothal otherwise known from Persian Gulf ports of Bahrain and Failaka and from Mesopotamia provides convincing proof of sea trade. Such trade and cultural ties continued after the Aryan ascendency in the subcontinent. Assyrian influences in the form of remarkable resemblances of archaeological finding in Balochistan also point out to the fact that Balochistan had been linked through some trade with Assyrian cities. [48] The Makkuran coast must have been used as the nucleus of trade and communication between India and the Middle East and between the Middle East and Central Asian countries.[49] Balochistan had also its trade relations with

---

47 Ibid. p.36.

48 Thomas Holdich, The Gates of India: Being an Historical Narrative, (First Published, London 1877). Reprinted, Goshae Adab, Quetta 1977, p.54.

49 Ibid.

its immediate neighbors, Afghanistan, Sindh and Persia. Such trade most probably was not regulated by any inter-governmental formal agreements. Goods were sent through caravan routes from various points in Balochistan to Kandahar, Ghazni, and Kabul and also the route from Kasarkand and Chahbar, and Noshki to Sistan and Khurasan was in use. Another track existed through Kerman, Sistan, and Helmand. Although it is not clear whether Mula or Bolan passes had been used as trade passes connecting India with Persia and the Middle East, the possibility cannot be ruled out altogether.

Balochistan always has fluctuating relations with India and Persia. It had changed masters not infrequently. Various parts of it were dominated by many empires in different stages of history. The present eastern Balochistan to the Indus was a part of the seventh Satrapy of Achaemenid Empire during the period of Darius (521-485 B.C), Sistan and western Makkuran was the fourteenth Satrapy, while eastern Makkuran and Southern Balochistan were included in the seventeenth Satrapy. It remained under Persians till 330 B.C. when the Greek acquired the area and remained under the Seleucid Empire till 305 B.C. Balochistan subsequently came under the Mauryan Indian Kingdom from 305 B.C. It was dominated by Kusanas Emperor, Kanisk, from 78 to 103 A.D. It was under the Scythians (78-200 A.D) and Sassanids (224-651 A.D) A part of Balochistan was under the Hephthalite Turks (470-520 A.D). The Kings of Sindh extended their influence into some parts of western Balochistan around 6th and 7th century A.D.

Another important point which should be taken into account is that some peoples with a distant culture living in the region at the time of the Baloch advent must have had their cultural impacts on the newcomers. As regards Medes, Parthians, and Sassanians, their cultural influence on the Baloch is fairly visible.[50] Some historical evidence suggests that the Medes and Jats were inhabiting the eastern part of Balochistan before the Baloch came into Gedrosia and further east. These peoples may not altogether have been eliminated by the invading forces. Therefore, there may have been an admixture of original inhabitants of the area reinforced by further immigration and assimilation either way since the second half of the second millennium B.C.

---

50 . Charles Masson, Narrative of Jouny to Kalat, (First pulished, London 1883) Reprinted by Indus publications, Karachi, 1976, pp. 431-432.

The archaeological findings must help to have some idea regarding the ancient peoples of Balochistan. Although it alone could by no means be the basis of reliable historical inferences, however; they offer certain evidence upon which further studies on socio-cultural traditions of the peoples of a certain region could be made. The conjectural evidence so far available from excavations, if taken together, suggest a definite pattern in the approaches and religious outlook of the ancient people of the region. It may be pointed out that archaeological discoveries have established a nearer relationship of the peoples of Balochistan throughout primitive epochs with the peoples of Indus Valley. It is also believed that some of the Baloch fighters were present in the Macedonian and Greek forces during the Greek supremacy of Central Asia and Iranian Plateau. Some religious thoughts of the ancient people of central Balochistan, especially the people of Naal in Jahlawaan, had a marked similarity with those of the Indus people. Another interesting aspect is that the people of Balochistan had cultural affinity among them also. Articles found in Killi Gulamahmad, a few miles from Quetta, have resemblances in style and pattern with the things found in Surab.

All these discoveries have established that Balochistan passed through the Stone and Bronze Ages. The material finds in Naal and Surab and also discoveries in Mehergad represent a fairly widespread level of cultural achievement and also indicate that Balochistan served as an intermediary between the cultures of South Asia, Middle East, and the Indus Valley. Remains in Mahergad, however, are understood to belong to Neolithic era some seven thousand years B.C. Therefore, the Baloch after their migration to these areas must have been influenced to a certain degree by the ancient peoples of the area.

We cannot rule out the Greek cultural impact on Balochistan which was under the Greeks for nearly twenty-five years. The language did not disappear soon after Alexander's (356 -323 B.C) departure or Gupta's acquiring of Balochistan, the Indus Valley and part of Afghanistan from General Seleucus in 305 B.C. Greek cultural influences remained in the area. Its language was spoken in the Indus Valley as late as the middle of the first century after the Christ. It indicates that the Greek settlements existed and possibly reinforced till a later period.[51] However, it is difficult to strictly judge the degree of

---

51 .Thomas Holdich, Op Cit, pp.21-22.

influences of Greek civilization as a whole on the Baloch as one can not be sure of the exact locations and settlements of the Baloch tribes at the time of Greek power in the region.

It is for certain that the Baloch culture is not totally devoid of Middle Eastern imprints. But this does not provide any base for the suggestion that the Baloch were Semites. Factors mentioned above which resulted in leaving a mark on Baloch traditions must be kept in view while analyzing the Baloch culture which is overwhelmingly Central Asian in its essence and Aryan by racial or linguistic affiliation. Great dissimilarities and fundamental differences in social and cultural outlook are visible between the ancient Semites and the Baloch. Among the Baloch, the system and manner of punishment had not been decapitation as it was in vogue among the Semites. The Mosaic Law is full of the mention of punishment of death. The principal mode of execution being stoning which later on was also sanctified by Arabian Islam for certain offenses had no acceptance among the Baloch. Similarly, burning alive was probably practiced and was a form of punishment sanctioned by Mosaic Law and used for incendiaries. Throwing the criminal from a rock was also a Semitic way of punishment.

Yet another important cultural innovation among the Semites was sacred or religious prostitution. This custom was practiced in the great Temple of Venus of Babylus where people performed ceremonies in the memory of Adonis who was believed to have been killed by a wild boar. The women had to cohabit with strangers.[52] Among the people of Israel, prostitution existed throughout the historical period of the Old Testament and appears to have been an accepted social norm. Among the various cult groups in Canaan and Israel, the temples of the different deities, all had their compartments of *q'deshah* or sacred whores.[53] Sacred prostitution was practiced also in Egypt where harlots were attached to temples, particularly those of god Amon.[54] Another widespread phenomenon of the ancient world which existed in Babylon was the case of eunuch priests, the religious transvestism that is when a priest or a devotee assumed woman's clothing. This ancient

---

52 . Fernando Henrique, Prostitution and Society: A survey, Mac gibbon kee, London, 1962, p.26.

53 .Ibid. p.33.

54 .Ibid. p.330.

custom which was in vogue among the Semites later found its way into the Middle Ages among the Muslim rulers as a proper household institution of eunuchs.[55]

The sacred harlotry has its reminiscence in the Beduin custom in Yemen and Haadremaut and which developed as a form of hospitality,[56] having nevertheless definite links with ancient forms of sacred prostitution which, it was believed helped the fertility of soul and of man. This sexual benevolence was still there till 18th century among the el-Merekede branch of the Asyr Tribes.[57] Its benign form, characteristic of the Mehra tribes of southern Arabia in the fourteenth century, can be said to have developed into a practice of sexual hospitality where a wife, daughter, or some female relative was placed at the disposal of a guest. It appears to have been widespread among a number of different tribes. Even the revolutionary wave of Islam appears to have had a little effect among the Arabs who were reluctant to give up many ancient customs verging on prostitution which they possessed since ancient times.[58] The tenacious character of religious prostitution was there even in the sacred rites of the *Kaaba* in Mecca. Some of the Banu Amir women used to perform the *thawaaf*, the circumambulation of *Kaaba* and the sacred black stone in Mecca in a naked state. Vestiges of this type of prostitution have lingered on till recently in Syria and elsewhere. A deviant Muslim Sect, the Ali Ullaheeahs of Kerun, indulged in a type of ritual promiscuity. At their annual feasts, women took off their clothes and the men paired off with them indiscriminately. in Mecca itself, as late as the nineteenth century, some of the women intoxicated by the holiness of pilgrims would copulate with the Faithfuls.[59]

There are quite a few historical indications that some form of prostitution also existed in India before the Aryan invasion. The story of the conception and birth of Birghatamas in *Mahabharata* shows that prostitution may have been practiced. It also appears that a form of paternal polyandry was in vogue. That is to say, brothers would

---

55 .Ibid. p.36.

56 The Uch-Majlis of the Paktoons, who claim a Semitic descent, in its earlier form must have had similar links with prostitution, religious or social.

57 .Ibid. p.337.

58 Ibid. p.335-337.

59 .Ibid. p.336.

keep one wife in common. The remnants of such practices in some other forms still exist in Punjab and many other areas in spite of the passage of time. Some other references in classical Hindu literature also show that some kind of prostitution existed. The *Samayamatrika* by *Kshemendra* is a biography of a courtesan, narrating her various experiences in various situations. From *Kautilya* and *Vatsyana* it could be seen that prostitution was there in ancient India.[60]

The Baloch always despised prostitution. It has never been an accepted social norm among the Baloch at any stage of history.

Another point which should not be discounted is that the Aryan came from a cold region of the Caspian, while Semites belonged to hotter places. Therefore, the Baloch has been preserving of a dress suitable for colder areas- a long shirt, big trouser and a large *paag* (turban). Many among the Baloch still have their houses open to the east. It may be due to the fact that they perhaps unconsciously are keeping the tradition of respect towards the sun which was revered by them in ancient past, or due to their habits of the cold Caspian region. Little over a span of three millennium years when they first started moving and settled in the hot regions of Iranian plateau and areas adjacent to the subcontinent, their cultural pattern in matters of dress and tastes must have undergone considerable changes. But whatever little evidence can be found, should be viewed with scientific objectivity. Similarly, one must not disregard the fact that there was a long line of Semitic prophets and religious reformers throughout the ages which must have resulted in a general religious tendency among the Semites and a refined approach towards God and the universe. This is evident from the Old Testament. The Aryans, or for that matter Central Asian peoples, had fewer reformers or religious preachers. Most of the Aryan people including the Baloch have still preserved their primitive cults in most respects. The Baloch still adopt names of animals, plants, colors, and even parts of the body, which was not in vogue among the Semites perhaps due to their religious outlook. The Baloch had always one-word names such as Gwahraam, Honnakk, Kiyya, Baahud, etc., however, there are absolutely no traces of any Semitic names among the ancient Baloch.

Physical traits or biological growth; language; folklore and literature; religion and mythologies; social and political institutions;

---

60 Ibid. pp. 153-157.

cultural affinity; geography and history are important factors in determining a people's racial or ethnic origin. With the analyses of these factors, although, the Baloch might have assimilated some of the linguistic and societal values, it becomes clear that there is no resemblance of the Baloch with Semites and they definitely belong to those groups of tribes who migrated from central Asia some three thousand years ago. It is now a consensus opinion among the researchers that the Baloch belongs to the family of those tribes who were speaking Indo-European languages.

THREE

THE BALOCH CULTURE

Culture manifests itself in history and philosophy, language and literature. It has its roots in customs, traditions, manners, laws, institutions, beliefs, and rituals, modes of worship and likes and dislikes. It is thus the historical manifestation of the will, aspiration, values, and spirit of a people, a vigorous unifying force within, cementing the traditional bonds of love and oneness.

Influences of culture upon human behavior and its powerful stimulations on individuals can hardly be overemphasized. It has a vast field and a varied role in human conduct; from checking the sex urge and achieving permanent celibacy to causing a person to shoot himself or someone else to wipe out a stain of dishonor. Culture exists in a natural habitat. The environment plays an important role in shaping many cultural temperaments, forbidding or encouraging the acquisition of certain habits. Climatic conditions have often led to more subtle adaptation in the cultural life of a community or people.

Every culture must have living ideas, some cardinal points to sustain and inspire. The political entity or a national identity is quite inconceivable without cultural existence. It is the cultural personality or the historical essence which gives birth to the political hypothesis of a people. Therefore, the first campaign launched by alien rulers against a people would always be on the cultural front which would take the form of a cruel and persistent war of resistant by a people against a politically and economically dominating power. What is termed as 'cultural oppression' is attempted mostly through falsification and misrepresentation of national history. The traditional institutions and values, social and political organizations are undermined and ridiculed to achieve, at the first instance, a gradual value re-orientation of those people. Everything which is connected with a people's past is dubbed as 'out-dated' and 'reactionary.' Other dubious tactics are employed including systematic condemnation of the entire social structure.

The Baloch culture and traditions have been subjected purposely to a dishonest analysis by those with whom the Baloch have been in constant conflict. Their socio-political institutions which are based largely on tribalism, like the most peoples in their transitional period of socio-economic development, are the main targets. The Baloch political system of the past has been portrayed as a permanent curse which decimated their vigor and vitality.[1] The history of the Baloch Confederacy at Kalat is termed to be the history of intrigues, feuds and tribal jealousies, the entire reign as anarchic and Machiavellian in its competitive ingenuity of misdeeds.[2] The prominent Baloch personalities were regarded as criminals,[3] unbounded by any principles[4], morally corrupt and deeply parochial.[5] The Baloch social practices were portrayed as barbaric, based on class differentiation; the social structure as outdated and full of evils.[6] It was mentioned by some writers that a person was said to be considered a true Baloch when he first committed some heinous crime and withstood some barbaric test of chivalry before he was recognized as an enterprising individual[7] and remains a threat and a permanent danger to another Baloch.[8] Not only this, a big segment of the Baloch people, the Brahui-speaking tribes were identified as Dravidians and their culture said to be inferior to the other Baloch tribes.[9] Khanate rule

---

1   Muhammad Sardar Khan Baloch, *The Great Baloch*, Balochi Academy, Quetta 165, p.77.

2   Muhammad Sardar Khan Baloch, *History of Baloch Race and Balochistan, Process Pakistan*, Karachi, 1958, p.120.

3   Charles Masson, Op. Cit. p.421.

4   Muhammad sardar Khan Baloch, *A Literary History of Balochis1*, Balochi Academy, Quetta, I.P.35.

5   Charles Masson, Op. Cit. p.357.

6   Muhammad Sardar Khan Baloch, *History of Baloch Race and Balochistan*, p, 189

7   Ibid, p.178.

8   Muhammad Sardar Khan Baloch, *The Great Baloch*, p.81.

9   Muhammad Sardar Khan Baloch, *History of Baloch Race and Balochistan*, p.269

at Kalat has been described as the Brahui rule at the cost of Balochi-speaking people, and that the Brahuis enjoyed more status than other tribes during the Khanate; ravishing the verdant fields and property of the neighboring tribes with least heed paid to the law of the land.[10] To make the matter of the Baloch origin more confused, it was concluded that the Baloch feel that they are an esteemed race; and are descendants of the Chaldeans who founded the world's first great civilization; and the Baloch are racist and are prone to under esteem all races save the Semites.[11] To further divide the Baloch, it was also claimed that among the Baloch only a particular tribe, *Rind*, represents the Baloch in all aspects and were supposed to be the best representatives of all Baloch virtues and vices.[12]

All this is a misrepresentation of Baloch history and culture. It aimed at pooh-poohing and depreciating an ancient people and sowing seeds of permanent discord among its various tribes. It was a calculated move to deface its culture, a vicious stratagem to leach the substance of devotion, bravery, and honor from it and devoid the society from its time-honored values, its essence or rationale. The effects of this systematic fabrication of the Baloch social and historical values is that their cultural traditions are bearing the weight of alien pressures in an intensely crude form. This has resulted in disarray and chaos in their social structure. The Baloch are being compelled to consider afresh their political choices in the countries which are controlling their land and people. For the youths, it appears very difficult to evolve a balance between national aspirations and sometimes promised rights in even ideal socio-political arrangements. In this perspective, they are confronting mighty forces to defend their national identity and to gain a place of respect in the community of nations which they feel is being denied.

The Balochi language which is an inseparable part of culture and which represents the true historical and cultural personality of the people, is being corrupted[13] in an effort to erase its true character, and

---

10   Ibid. p.172

11   Muhammad Sardar Khan Baloch, *The Great Baloch*, p.80

12   Muhammad Sardar Khan Baloch, *A Literary History of Balochis*, Vol. 1, Balochi Academy, Quetta, P.73

13   A survey conducted by the author of words and phrases used in Balochi programmes of Radio Pakistan, Afghan and Iranian state owned Radio,

if possible, replace it within a few generations with the language of the rulers, in the classical pattern of when a particular language was made to drive all other languages in an empire and replaced them by the tongue of the masters.

In the pugnacious maneuvers against indigenous culture, an active part is always played by the so-called intellectuals from among those peoples who are pushed through in the social and intellectual circles by the rulers. To establish their credibility with the masters, they misrepresent the cultural heritage of their own people and try to create confusion among the raw minds who start to develop complexes and sometimes a strong dislike towards their own traditions. It is not only the Persians or the Arabs or the English who tried to write the Baloch history accordingly to their own hegemonic needs, not surprisingly a great many "historians" have emerged within the last few decades writing on Baloch people. They are following the examples set by the British intelligence officers in the guise of travelers or later administrators of occupied Balochistan. They are faithfully obeying the dictates of the present controllers of the Baloch land in falsifying the Baloch history and making confusing conclusions of their "purposely designed research works".

No sincere efforts were made to highlight the Baloch culture in its true spirit and study its deep-rooted institutions objectively. A superfluous approach was adopted about the uselessness and rigidity of such institutions and their futility in the modern era. Among the Baloch themselves, unfortunately, there was no Herodotus or Xenophon. Information about them emanated from its enemies who twisted its history to suit political exigencies with the result that the Baloch youths are completely unaware of their cultural traditions. Only a few writers have endeavored to present a correct picture of its culture and help in understanding it in its true historical perspective. But they have their pitfalls. They have based their notions entirely on Baloch traditions depicted mostly in poetry and some isolated historical events. They have also founded their theories on a few loan-words in Balochi language and bare names in genealogy or some cultural traits appearing to be common with certain peoples. Another fallacious

---

Kabul and Zahidan, and the Television Corporation of Pakistan for six months from August 1980 to February 1981 shows that more than seventy per cent of those are alien words used in-appropriately and very purposefully in Balochi.

approach of these writers is that they want to judge the primitive Baloch, their thoughts and behaviour against the background of the present socio-political and economic standards or on some other criteria,[14] with least regard to the fact that the approach of the ancient Baloch must have been conditioned by the limitations they faced, and which may not be in existence today. Today, we have sufficient authentic historical record to analyze and arrive at conclusions on various aspects of human endeavors, while the primitive man did not have sufficient means to know the past and benefit from such experience, except the events in the span of a few generations, at the most. Moreover, the important fact was conveniently disregarded that the Baloch history is not the description of some peninsula or river valleys; it is the history of a people wandering throughout their over 3,000 years of existence.

In spite of this systematic and well-planned campaign, the Baloch generally, have rejected frivolous notions about their history and have shown a marked contempt towards those mischievous theories. They are resisting cultural onsluaght[15] and are very slow in accepting cultural change and language transformation. But they are living in an era of constant change. Resistance to the cultural offensive may not be enduring indefinitely merely by force of national will. It is, however, true that many peoples survived foreign domination and kept their cultures intact. The Greeks survived centuries of Turkish overlordship; Kurds are keeping their traditions intact against the hostile Persians, Turk, and Arab cultures which have a dominating position by virtue of being the rulers of Kurdistan. The Hindus to a very large extent preserved their culture against hostile Muslims after the invasion of India by the Arabs in the early 8th century; so also did many other nations who remained under colonial powers. The Baloch also possess a great spirit of resistance and have been able to preserve their national

---

14 We have instances of judging civilizations and cultures of many ancient peoples by some alien standards. Earlier, Persian and Indian history and culture were tested by Greek or Roman standards. Civilizations which did not come to such arbitrary criteria were usually regarded inferior.

15 Readers are referred to articles/write-ups on various aspects of Baloch culture in Pakistan newspapers and journals. The so-called Baloch intellectuals are usually engaged for the purpose. Programmes being sponsored by state-owned Pakistan Television and Broadcasting Corporations are willful mis-representation of Baloch culture.

identity since the Great Pogrom during the reign of the Persian Monarch, Khusrow-I, the Anushervan, in the face of disastrously unfavorable circumstance. The other people in this respect are only the Jews, a marvelous people who have not only managed to preserve their identity but established their national state, Israel after 2000 years of stateless wanderings.

However, in a world of so-called cultural affinity based mostly on geography and history, it will be too naïve an assertion that the Baloch culture has not undergone variations or has remained static. It has been in the process of continual transformation. Changes, particularly political domination, wars and social upheavals of various epochs have brought considerable permutations in the nature of customs and traditions of many peoples and sometimes replaced them by a set of another. Culture of victorious peoples had always a sway slowly over the culture of the vanquished. Nevertheless, an analytical study of other cultures in almost similar conditions shows that the Baloch had preserved their cultural equivalence remarkably well. This may have been possible due to comparative inaccessibility of their area to foreign domination. There is also some cultural diversity among the Baloch themselves for the obvious reason that as an unsettled and wandering peoples at times, interchanges amongst its various branches were quite difficult. Many tribes were isolated from other tribes for long periods, nevertheless, they resisted any marked deviation and maintained their cultural personality against heavy odds.

No culture could be judged arbitrarily without taking into account many geopolitical and religious factors. Every culture must have some instinctive base which must also have some religious sanctions. Most of them continued due to their effectiveness for the society even after the religious base has been undermined. Therefore, the substantial cultural diversity throughout the world must be viewed with proper historical understanding, An Englishman who shakes hands while greeting another or a Polynesian who pressed noses has no cultural superiority to a Frenchman who embraces or kisses on both cheeks. A Muslim woman who veils her face has no spiritual, moral or cultural excellence over an African who leave her breasts uncovered and on some religious occasions goes even naked. Still more, polygamy is considered obnoxious among many people while it is widely practiced in many countries with religious authority. In some cultures, pre-marital sex relations are not considered a sin while many people uphold the chastity of both sexes before marriage. Celibacy is thought in many societies as a highly spiritual and moral act while others almost despise it. The Baloch regarded the institution of prostitution or trade in sex as most degrading and essentially evil, while most ancient peoples practiced it and among the remnants of some of the ancient peoples in the subcontinent it may still be an accepted social norm in some distinct forms the ancient custom which requires a woman by virtue of her marriage to one man to copulate with his close relatives. The Baloch truthfulness and profound sincerity cannot be regarded to be merely a primitive innocence. The Baloch have never been appreciative of those who are deceitful and cunning and whose culture has no strict rules to disapprove it. Many people never keep promises, and there is nothing obligatory on them to keep a promise which has been imperfectly developed and where acts of flagrant perfidity are usually mentioned without blame and sometimes described with approbation.[16]

The Baloch customs and their collective approach was entirely based on an intense feeling for good human conduct prescribed by society. Those by no means could be regarded as circumstantial conjunctions of individuals but were always determined and maintained through a constant social process. A Baloch was brought up in a peculiar social and cultural environment. He was constantly taught and reminded from the early childhood of the role he was to play and the imperatives of the tribal society. Even the games of his early age always touched the tribal manners and the onerous responsibilities ahead. When grown up, he became part and parcel of the tribal structure with a strong tendency to adhere strictly to the tribal ethos.

The Baloch moral philosophy had always been centered on what they considered good or evil, judging by their own social standards. A Baloch was obliged to follow what was regarded as proper and benefiting. Everybody was expected to play a definite role. He was always watched in his actions. A Baloch was expected to follow in individual and collective life the tribal code of conduct which was readily obeyed by all ostensibly without any objection. No one would

---

16 Among the ancient Greek, dishonesty was sometimes appreciated. The deceitful cunningness was favorably mentioned in their classical literature. The perfidious manipulation of Ulysses in the Homeric poems appears as a virtue of the same rank with the sagacity of Nestor, the steadiness of Hector and bravery of Achilles.

challenge the reasonableness or expediency of customs. The Baloch never easily accepted alien manners. Even after accepting the Arabian religion of Islam, they usually preferred their own way of life and its customs always proved stronger than the laws of the new faith.

He was truthful and honest. He believed in social equality, exceptionally brave, was ready to protect and fight for his *Baahot*. (A Baahot is a person who has been given protection or asylum by a Baloch) He was hospitable and helpful. He was proud and conscious of his noble birth. He never married into an alien caste and always desired to maintain his racial purity. He never tolerated insults. Female dishonor could be washed out only with blood. Miserliness and avarice were equally damnable. Celibacy or barrenness for the woman was strongly disliked. Only among non-Baloch in the Baloch society, especially *Sayyads* who considered themselves of Arab origin celibacy was observed. The Baloch considered a woman without children as quite useless. Being barren *"Sant"* for a lady had always been a bad connotation. A man who does not marry is still looked down upon and called a *Lund* having derogatory connotations. Suicide was thought to be an act of cowardice. Loss of status in the community or violation of taboos did rarely bring self-punishment. Sometimes, however, he killed himself to remove an honor stain. According to some traditions, *Shey Mureed* afflicted ninety-nine *daags* (Marks made by branding) on his body, made through burning rods as a mark of repentance and consequent punishment for giving up Haani-his fiancé. Beggary was disapproved. It was considered as a big insult. The old and disabled were to be looked after by their relatives. Those who had no relatives were looked after by neighbors or were given aid at the time of harvests or on ceremonial occasions. It was always against the profound sense of honor of a Baloch to beg for his or her livelihood.

Truthfulness and honesty were regarded as the best virtues. The hero in all stories is deeply honest and truthful in the face of even compromising situations. Moreover, he is of noble birth possessing the greatest human qualities. We come across many instances in the folk literature of many peoples when the hero may sometime tell a lie to keep himself out of impending danger or situation beyond his control. But the Baloch always tells the truth whatever may be the consequences. Sometimes a person acting against the general principles and asking the help of a miser or coward is shown repenting. Bravery is the highest quality. Courageous people usually come out from dangerous situations and impossible tests. The forms of these tests are varied which usually include a fight with monsters or bringing things or objects beyond ordinary human reach. At times the brave persons get the daughters of the kings in marriage or other things after coming out of the tests of bravery. Mir Chaakar's fight with an elephant and his riding an untamed horse is the theme of a Balochi poem. He had undergone these tests of bravery to please Sultan Husain Mirza of Herat whose help he sought to avenge the Nali defeat. [There is however no evidence of Mir Chaakar's travel to Herat to solicit the help of sultan against Mir Gwahraam except a poem which narrates the details of Mir Chaakar's journey to Herat where he stayed as a state guest]. The Sultan before granting his request for military assistance put him to test by asking him to ride an untamed horse and fight an elephant. Mir Chaakar did both successfully. (Putting any person to tests who sought help in any form was, however, never approved in Baloch traditions.) All these events must be imaginary and without sound historical proofs, but they show clearly the honor or status the Baloch accorded to a brave person. Similarly, Mir Hammal's fight with a lion which is the theme of another Balochi poem may be fictitious, but it fully shows that bravery was the highest honor among the Baloch. They always revered the brave and hated the cowards who had no role to play in society.

The Baloch was deeply proud and egoistic. There are instances in history that to boost the individual or tribal ego, he took actions or made vows quite inconsistent with general practices. Vows made by Chaakar, Haibithaan, Jaado, Mureed, and Sumael-e-Haaro apparently had no rationale; but such instances were considered appropriate in boosting the extreme sense of their pride. The killing of its non-combatant women folk in order to avoid their being dishonored by the enemy is a glaring example. The Baloch who fought to defend Multan under Hendo, killed their women because they feared that they might be molested in case of their defeat which was imminent. In 1539 during the Mughal-Suri conflict in the subcontinent, Multan came under a few Baloch tribes. Sher Shah Suri sent Haibath Khan Niazi, the Governor of Punjab to subdue the rebellious Baloch under the command of Hendo and Bakhshu. The Baloch killed most of their women themselves. In the battle, next day three hundred Baloch fought the invading forces and were routed. Their leaders were taken as prisoners.[17]

---

17   .Muhammad Sardar Khan, *A Literary History of Balochis*, Vol. I, p.61

The Baloch had a penetrating sense of national justice. Throughout history, they never accepted any subservient position and insulting domination. They always fought the forces of exploitation, regardless of the consequences. The first national disaster which betook the Baloch for which we have historical record was their quarrel with Anushervan, the Iranian Monarch of Sassanid dynasty, who ordered an armed excursion into Baloch area on a large scale. The exact nature of the conflict is not known, but it must have been the result of undue interference in their social and religious affairs by the Iranian government. The *Shahnama* maintains that the Baloch created anarchy in their territory by engaging in acts of robbery against the caravans; this, however, does not carry much weight. There must be other political or religious reasons. The Baloch preferred to give battle to the mighty forces of the Persian Empire than to surrender or accept any interference in their social or religious affairs. Siyah Sawaar, the Baloch leader who defected from Iranian forces to join the invading Arab army could be cited as another example of the Baloch sense of independence. He negotiated a truce with Abu Musa, the Commander of the Arab army, at Kalbaniyah. The conditions put forward by Siyah Sawaar included the acceptance by the Arabs of the provisions that the Baloch should be given free choice, where ever they liked to live and league with tribes they chose,[18] and that Arabs would not interfere in their internal affairs. These conditions were ultimately accepted by Caliph Omar. The Baloch did not accept the hegemony of notorious plunderer Sultan Mahmud of Ghazna in their internal affairs and offered fierce resistance to the armies led by Mahmud's son, Masud, at a time when resistance to the might of Sultan Mahmud was unthinkable.

Even among themselves the Baloch never tolerated supremacy of one tribe over the other. The Rind-Lashaar conflict which ended in nine major battles,[19] over a period of thirty years beginning most

---

18   Muhammad Sardar Khan, *The Great Baloch*, pp, 20-21

19   Nine major battles were fought between Rind and Lashaar. The last three were decisive. Lashaar were defeated at Gajaan, while Rind were routed at Nali after nearly five years. The last battle against the Lashaar was fought after much preparation by Mir Chaakar with the help of Shujuddin Zannun, the Arghun, who was ordered by the Khurasan ruler, Sultan Husain Mirza to help the Baloch chieftain. Lashaar were defeated. A large number of them migrated to Sind and Gujrat in India.

probably after 1450 A.D, resulted in the utter defeat of Lashaar and the consequent weakening of Rind power in Balochistan was the result of that Baloch uncompromising attitude and tribal ego. The Rind-Lashaar dispute apparently erupted when the Rind judges of a horse-race between Raamen Lashaar and Rehaan Rind allegedly favored the Rind contestee. The Lashaar could not tolerate this injustice; and while withdrawing killed the camels of Gohar, a *Baahot*, of Mir Chaakar Rind.[According to traditions, Raamen Lashaar and Rehaan Rind, both in their teens had a love affair with a cobbler's wife. It was agreed between them that the loser in the race had to forego his love for that woman].

Mir Naseer Khan's (ruled 1750-1794 A.D) conflict with Afghan king, Ahmed Shah Durrani, who was one of the greatest powers in Central Asia in the 18th century had also its genesis in the Baloch's extreme sense of pride. It was obvious that Naseer Khan by no means could withstand the Afghan ruler's onslaught if the situation had taken that turn, but he was determined to fight back.[20] Mir Mehraab Khan's

---

20 It is generally believed that the Afghan invasion of Kalat took place after Naseer khan interfered in Sindh affairs which was under Ahmad Shah Durrani. The Khan arrested Atar Khan, a nominee of Ahmad Shah in Sindh, who was defeated by the forces collected by Mian Ghulam Shah. The arrest took place at Kalat when Atar khan and his brother were on their way to Afghanistan to apprise the Shah of the Sindh situation. It is also believed that Naseer Khan thought that the time was opportune to declare his independence from Afghan hegemony at a moment when the Afghan armies in India had been routed and the Shah's prestige was at the lowest ebb in the country. Both the propositions appear baseless. Mir Naseer Khan was not unaware of the military strength of the Afghan king and knew that he could by no means repulse a military invasion on Kalat. He always honoured the treaties arrived at from time to time. Even the later Khans following the traditions and never violated any treaty commitments in spite of the fact that the Afghan rulers granted asylum to dissident Baloch Sardars and often encouraged them in their intrigues against various Khans. If Naseer Khan really wanted a conflict he could have taken steps in that direction by mobilizing the Baloch fighting men or at least by capturing Sibi which was militarily important and was under Afghan suzerainty. It also does not seem proper that Ahmed Shah declared war upon Kalat for the reason that Naseer Khan had arrested one of his representative in Sindh, Atar Khan. The fact most probably was that the Afghan ruler and some of his nobles interfered in Kalat affairs which was intolerable to the Khan and which resulted ultimately in war. Consequently a detachment of Afghan troops under Shah Wali, the Prime Minister of Afghanistan was

martyrdom had that swelling sense of national pride behind it. He fought against the invading British forces not because he was sure of his victory but because he considered it the only just way, and to show cowardice was inconceivable.[21] Mir Baloch Khan fought to the last in Gokprosh in 1898 against the British forces led by Captain Burnes despite the fact that he was deserted by his ally, the treacherous Sardar Mehraab Khan Gichki of Kech, and was sure of his defeat. He could have arrived at an agreement with the British Commander, but he preferred death upon a shameful surrender.

The events of the last decades show that the Baloch attitude towards many issues has not changed. The Baloch political struggle which often took the shape of the general resurrection, or more appropriately tribal wars, against the successive governments of Pakistan and Iran had the historical reality in the background that they are fiercely freedom-loving and intensely conscious of their

---

sent against Naseer Khan. The Khan defeated the Afghans near Mastung, thirty miles from shaal, the present day Quetta. Hearing this, Ahmad Shah marched in person at the head of a strong army. The Khan retreated to his capital Kalat which was besieged by the Afghan troops. The siege lasted for forty days. Finally, a negotiated settlement was reached between the two erstwhile allies and the Afghan troops withdrew.

21 During the first Anglo-Afghan war of 1839-41, the Balcoh tribesmen often ambushed British convoys of troops and supplies on their way to Afghanistan. The British suffered losses in men and material while passing through troublesome routes in Baloch territory. The British authorities regarded Mir Mehraab Khan, the Ruler of Kalat responsible for those attacks. Moreover, the British wanted to subjugate Kalat as a first step toward dominating Afghanistan in order to implement the foreign policy objectives enunciated in the so-called forward policy vis-a-vis Russia's territorial containment in Central Asia. For his part, the Khan did not discourage those raids on British troops because he considered the conquest of Afghanistan as the ultimate downfall of his Khanate. He had also rejected an earlier British proposal to meet the British supported Shah Shujah. The Khan thought that such a meeting could have been interpreted as recognizing Shah Shujah's claim as the Afghan king.

As the Khan was treaty bound not to interfere in the internal affairs of Afghanistan, he refused to meet Shah Shujah, which further antagonized the British authorities. After the British mission of ousting Amir Dost Muhammad in Kabul, the British turned their attention towards Kalat. Sir Thomas Wilshire brigade was diverted from Quetta to attack Kalat which was besieged. After an hand to hand fight on 13th November 1839, the Khan was killed and his capital captured.

national identity. In the Baloch conflicts against these governments, there is least doubt that they are not a good match in armament, resource or manpower to the modern armies of these countries; but they are reluctant to give in and adamant to fight because in Baloch social ethos it is inconceivable to compromise on what they regard as their inalienable rights.

These national values are deeply rooted. The Baloch folk-literature provides a vast field to analyze the true essence of their socio-cultural ethos. Folk stories or proverbial sayings play a major role in depicting the socially accepted norms. For example, the Baloch considered treachery as immoral and vicious. In many stories, the treacherous person is portrayed as either a low-caste or ultimately shown as a fallen villain. Respectful Sardars and their trusted comrades have never been shown as perfidious. Betrayal to public or family cause or to a friend is not only strongly disapproved of but persons who did so always met their doom unceremoniously.

The Baloch settlements

A Baloch lived in a large and open house with his family and flock usually within the same premises. Houses were built around a wooden framework with long slender poles, bent and curved towards each other. For temporary abode, tents were erected which were made from animal wool. Huts and gidaans were also made used for the temporary abode and the materials obtained from various plants were installed. He was absolute in his family, while his social life centered around the leading men whose houses were the main community centers.

Names and titles

Traditionally the name of a child was chosen a few days after birth, mostly on the sixth. The child was given the name of some worthy forefather who was not alive. But in the first instance, he was given an alternate name. As the Baloch had great respect for their departed elders, they gave names to the children formally but in the meantime, alternate names were chosen because the children by those names would be receiving rebuke which was considered an insult to those names and always avoided.

Among the Baloch, names were considered magically effective and had to have some bearing on the person. The Baloch borrowed names from animals, trees, plants, colors and even part of the body. Names were also derived from the name of weekdays, Doshambe (Monday), Shambe (Saturday), Chaarshambe (Wednesday), Jumma (Friday) were the common names. Other name were Pullien (Flowery), Kahoor (Prosopis Spicigera,) Chegird (Acacia), Kunar (ZizyphisJujuba) Shinzi (Camelthorn), Gazzi, (Tamarisk), Suhail (Canopus), Gwani (Pistachio), Gushu (Long-eared), Baahad (Arm), Kambar (Black and white), Siyaho (Blackish), Mazaar (Tiger), Sher (Lion). They had a one-word name like Honakk, Kiyya, Bijjar, Gwahraam, Baalaach, Haibithaan.

Abbreviated forms of the name of ordinary people, *nemnaam*, were also in vogue. Gwahru for Gwahraam, Haibuk for Haibithan, etc. The words Mir, Waja, Kahoda were added out of courtesy. These gentleman's prefixes sometimes became a part of the name. For women, Bibi or Baanuk was always added to the name of good birth. Their names were derived from various sources depicting beauty, honor, and soberness. Maahu (Like moon). Sangin (extremely reasonable, weighty), Sharri (Righteousness), Thilu (golden or like gold), Baanadi (lady- lord).

Father's name was sometimes added to the actual name, as Chaakar-e-Shaihakk (Chaakar son of Saihakk) or Haibithaan Muraad (Haibithaan son of Muraad). This practice most probably has crept into Baloch culture through Arabic influence at a much later stage.

Costumes: Dress-Jewellery

The Baloch wore a *jaamag*, a long shirt, down to heels and baggy trousers; a turban (*paag*), and shoes made of leather or *sawaas*, made from the leaves of Mideterrian dwarf palm *(pish)*. The jaamag had side pockets. They always tried to wore white dresses. Overcoat or waistcoat (*Kaba*), which was usually embroidered in different colors was used by noblemen. *Shaal* or *chaadir* which was a mark of distinction was used by elderly persons who wrapped it around the waist and knees for a particular sitting position in Balochi Diwaan called *kamarzani*. Socks have also been in use.

Women wore loose shirts or gowns and trousers. In Ancient times, women used only a large loose shirt which covered her from neck to the feet and usually did not wear trousers. The gown was ornamented with a profusion of needlework of various matching colors. The lower part of the shirt had a large front pocket *(pandol)* which was also embroidered. She had a *chaadir or gushaan* (Large Scarf) on the head which also covered the neck and chest. women wore shoes and socks. Virgin and widows usually wore black *jaamag*; and among some tribes, widows used white, without any embroidery, while a married woman used various colors, the favorite being red. The married old women sometimes used a black shirt without embroidery. They did not use any jewelry or ornaments. If a widow used embroidered dress, it was a clear indication that she intended to remarry.

In matters of dress, the Baloch were sometimes influenced by their neighbors. In Sistan about a century back, the Baloch wore Persian frock-coat and trousers. The female dress had a marked similarity with the Persians. In Sind and Punjab, the Baloch occasionally wore the dress of indigenous people. The women, however, maintained their dress in its original shape and style.

Both men and women had long hair. Hair was usually braided was parted in the center of the forehead. This separation was called *giwaar*. The men usually had a single braid while for women the hair was beautifully managed in two and left down back. Hair extensions were also in vogue.

Women in some areas used *aamad*, the black tooth paint. The head was usually bound with a fillet or black stuff or silken cloth. *Teetuk* or tattooings were made on women's forehead and cheeks, especially of newly married girls.

The Baloch use of jewelry has a close affinity with the Aryan's traced from the archaeological findings. The Baloch thought that garments or jewelry could ward off evil and protect persons from vicious elements. Such beliefs also existed among most other peoples. The Baloch believed that some evil forces who were in search of an opportunity to harm human being could be checked by the use of jewelry or some metallic articles. The bridegroom beside his usual ornaments, such as a sword, had some hidden object on his person during the marriage ceremony, at least, the first night of the marriage.

The women wore *durr* (earrings), *pulu or pulluk* (nose rings) *haar or thouk* (necklace), *mundrik* (rings in hands and foot fingers), *Sanga or taal* (bracelets), *Baahuband or baahink* (armlets). Ornaments of various kinds were fixed on the hair including Choti-pull, Moudi, which were fixed in the hair near the back. *Taali* was added as a hair extension.

Ceremonies

The occasion of the birth of either a male or a female child was marked with much music and singing. The womenfolk attended the mother for seven nights and sang *sipath or naazink*, literally meaning a song of praise. Food and sweets were prepared and distributed among neighbors and needy families. The birth of a boy was greeted with greater rejoicing than the birth of a girl. In some tribes, no ceremonies were performed on the birth of a girl, while among other tribes usual ceremonies were performed from birth to death. The ceremonies included the birth ceremony, *Shashigaan* (selecting a name on the sixth day), *burruk* (circumcision), *paadgaami* (the ceremony marking the first step taken by the child) and *shalwaar* (the first wearing of trousers by the child), etc.

Marriages which generally took place after puberty were performed with ceremonies which included music, dancing, and distribution of food or almsgiving. The girl was usually a few years junior to the boy. Marriage was arranged mostly to a closely knit family. Expenses of food prepared on either side was borne by the bridegroom. To meet the expenses and the amount of *labb* (the price for a bride), the family members of the bridegroom collected *bijjaari*, that was donation or subscriptions from relatives and friends. Traditionally, everyone who was asked gave according to his means. Sheep, cows, goats or camels were also presented as *bijjaar*, Relatives of the bride also collected *bijjaar* called *giwaari* on the evening of the marriage ceremony.

The general characteristic of a wedding included negotiations by parents and other relatives. All details were agreed upon and the wedding was formalized later on. *Labb* was Fixed beforehand. Betrothal *(Saang or harbarsindi)*, was the first step. The marriage expenses *(pardaach)*, was given to the bride's family by the bridegroom.

Pardaach was paid in cash or kind before the marriage date. It also included embroidered clothes and other essential articles for the bride.

Saang was almost as absolute as the marriage itself. After the engagement, the parents of the girl were bound to give the hand of the lady to the person to whom she was betrothed. There was no backing out from either side save in exceptional circumstances. Only in rare cases, could the man forego his fiancé, *dishthaar.*

Saahbadal or system of exchange of girl between families without stipulations paid was also prevalent.[22] sometimes conditions were made that a daughter born of a marriage would be given to relations of the bride's parents. However, if there was a marked difference in the ages or personal attractions or any physical defect of would be bride and bridegroom, it would then be compensated in money by either side. Betrothal in childhood among close relatives was also common.

The date of marriage was usually announced well in advance and all the relatives and friends were duly informed. In former times, the invitation for participation was sent to the entire clan which then selected the individuals for taking parts in the ceremonies on their behalf. However, at a much later stage, the invitations were sent to individuals and family heads. The persons sent for inviting the people, *Lotuki*, included singers and dancers who started singing and dancing before entering a village. The party would then be feasted by the village headman before their return.

A few days before the event, a *Kaapar* or a large wooden tent was built, a few yards from the home of the bridegroom. In coastal areas, this temporary tent was called *mangeer* where more than one marriage ceremonies were performed. This was built for the occasion by the community under the supervision of the village headman. All ceremonies including dancing and singing were performed there. This would also serve as a guest house for visitors from the nearby villages. Among peculiar customs, *korag*, was most prominent. The bridegroom was taken a few furlongs outside the settlement as the word connotes most probably to the riverside, in the afternoon or mid-day, where arrangements were made for his bath and makeup. He would then mount on horseback or camel and was brought to *diwaanjaah* or *mangeer* amid much singing an dancing. The occasion is also marked with *theerandaazee* (archery) among the participants. Another peculiar

---

22 Balochistan Through Ages: A selection from Government Record, Vol: II Nesa Traders, Quetta, 1979, P.274

custom was that a week before the marriage, the girl was secluded from the rest of the family. Only the closest female relatives and friends could visit her. During this period she was briefed regarding her duties and responsibilities after marriage. After sunset, the bridegroom profusely arrayed, accompanied by close friends and relatives moved to the bride's house where proper arrangements were made for their food. The formal wedding was performed after the guests were feasted.

Burial Rites

Burial customs were very simple. There seems to be no desire to preserve the corpse because the Baloch never believed in an after-life though the bond between the living and the dead was never broken. The living did follow the principles which their forefathers pursued, but no tombs or any such conspicuous arrangements were made for the dead. It was believed that there was the end of the individual after death. However, it appears that in some early stages in history mainly through Buddhist metaphysical thoughts, the Baloch might have believed that the soul or the dead may continue to survive. Death according to the Baloch would not transform the human status which remained as whatever manner the person behaved during his life, and according to his social position. However, a great deal depended on the living relatives who would have earned a bad name for him, thus making his soul, uneasy and disapproving.

Baloch mourned the death of a person in a manner appropriate to the dead man's social position. Death of a hero or a Sardar was lamented for several days extending to forty days, the phenomenon is called *Purs*. Almost the entire tribe participated in the ceremonies which were always simple. On the death of a person, people gathered at the house of the deceased or that of the head of that family to express their sympathy to the dead man's relatives. Most people would come during the first few days. However, those who might have been on a journey or belonged to remote areas could visit the mourning family conveniently even after months. Contributions were offered by the people according to their means to support the family or in meeting the expenses on that occasion. The dead was praised for his good deeds. Generally, there were no *purs* for a person killed on the charges of adultery.

Death of women was also mourned. However, among some tribes, no *purs* was observed, and there was no mourning for women. The Bijjaraani clan of Mari tribe did not observe *purs* for women till recently. This was not an original Baloch practice and might have crept through alien customs.

A Baloch never wept or cried in public to mourn the death of his relative or friend. Weeping was considered the greatest weakness for him. He usually sat calmly well-dressed in a dignified manner. His expression of grief was always in an honorable way. According to some unsubstantiated traditions, on the eve of migration from Sibi to Punjab, Mir Chaakar Rind became emotional and tears came down his cheeks. He might have been thinking of the glorious old days when the Rind was the dominant power of eastern Balochistan but was being compelled to leave the area because of internal rivalry. But when he realized that he was being watched by his own servant he killed him instantly so that nobody could be a witness to his shedding tears which was a mark of weakness. If such emotional stages arose, a Baloch would cover his face with his turban or *chaadir* so that nobody could see him shedding tears.

Games

The leisure hours were spent in playing and gambling. The most favorite among the games for the adults was horse racing. Surprisingly quite a few games of sport developed any uniform rules or specifications to be organized on a vast scale as intertribal games, save the horse race and archery. Another important innovation was betting on the games by participants themselves or by onlookers. The games of chance which were prevalent in almost every ancient culture were also there in Baloch traditions. Lots were also cast not only as a favorite game of chance but also for ending disputes or dividing the property. There are scores of references in folk literature about people gambling, using their most valuable things at stakes.

Another phenomenon was that most of the games were not merely meant for sports; these, in fact, provided proper training for the individual to shoulder his responsibilities as a useful member of the tribe. For instance horse race and sports resembling polo or archery provided sound practical training for young men to participate in wars.

Indoor games included those which required considerable insight and planning stratagem.

Music and dances

The Baloch has a rich musical culture. His interest in music was profound. It is possible that like other civilizations, music among Baloch had functions connected with religion. However, its ecstatic and secular possibilities cannot be ruled out altogether even in the ancient time. The Baloch treated persons suffering from a type of psychological disorder *"Gwaath"* through music. The patients were called *Gwaathi*. Minstrels played music on *sorouz* and *thamburag* in a rhythmic and repeated way. When the music reached its climax the *gwaathi* started a relentless movement in a dancing pattern. This would continue for many hours until late at night. It was believed that music would construe some magical effect, and the disease which had been caused definitely by some evil forces would end.

Music had its importance on all occasions except death when the ceremonies were of a more solemn nature. Other accessions were marked with much singing and dancing. The Balochi *sur* or *raags* which is termed *Zaheerag* because of their general characterization of melancholy pattern could be categorized under two main heads: Balochi and Kurdi. All others which may be as many as twenty come under these heads. Under Balochi, comes its various branches: miedi gor-o-baam, mianag, ashrap-e-durra, and janozaami. Kurdi included Bashkard, Jahlawaani kurdi, Shahr kurdi, Salaath, and Tat. It may, however, be noted that the entire Balochi musical structure is based on Zaheerag. Some of the folk music appears to be somewhat different from it but in their formal structure, all musical *sur* or derivatives have their base in Zaheerag. Among the musical instruments nal, thamburag, chang, and sorouz were important.

Dances were always collective and associated with the group. There was no fiery manner of dance. Religious dances were not prevalent. However, in the more recent past, Zigry sect, among the Baloch, practiced a kind of religious dance called *chogaan*. It, however, varied much from classical temple dances of most ancient cultures.

The main dance was *do-chaapi* where men gathered and danced, clapping hands with the movement of the foot, neck, and head on rhythmic music on the drum, *dohl*. Any kind of dance apart from *do-chaapi* was not universal. Basically, it was for the enjoyment of performers and spectators. On many occasion, women moved in a circle clapping hands but without body movements such as *do-chaapi*. *Lewa*, *hambo*, and *latti* were also prevalent mostly through foreign influence. Lewa is supposed to be of Arabian origin, while latti and Hambo were clearly dances of the ancient indigenous people of Balochistan. Do-chaapi and other group dances were performed by all but individual dance performers always belonged to low-castes.

Drinks

Use of drinks and intoxicants, especially *Bang*, made from hemp leaves was common. We find many instances in Balochi poetry which indicate that this liquor was used by all Baloch of any means.

Trade and commerce

The Baloch seldom engaged in trade. It is something which did not behove an honorable Baloch. His profession was war and manly pursuits. Trade and commerce were always handled by non- Baloch or more recently, by Hindus and Afghans.

Haal

Haal was giving and receiving news when one chanced to meet another. It was an obligation, and always reciprocal. A person must communicate the latest happenings which may include the prices of essential goods in a nearby market or some events of a more serious nature. This helped in conveying the latest happenings in remote areas. When traveling in groups, the *haal* was given by the elderly person of noble birth. This was called *chehabar*. To reveal or receive haal was a mark of distinction.

Mesthaagi

Mesthaagi was the reward for giving good news such as the birth of a son, news of the arrival of a lost relative or report of a victory in the battle. It was appropriate and according to the good news conveyed. In her reflective imagination, Haani said she would give in *mesthaagi*, her son, her entire belongings and even Mir Chaakar, her hated husband, to the person who may bring the good news of Shey Mureed, her ex-fiance.[23] *Mesthaagi* could be in cash or in kind, and the social status of the giver of the news was also counted in apportioning *Mesthaagi*.

Diwaan

The Baloch had an open society with its unique characteristic of equality and freedom. Every Baloch was expected to be an active

---

23 Haani a beautiful lady, was engaged in her childhood to one Shey Mureed. Mir Chaakar, the Rind chief who liked her, wanted her hand. But since she was already engaged he resorted to a stratagem. Once in the Diwaan he made a vow that he would never tell a lie under any circumstances. Haibithaan and Jaado, the two nobles also made vows. Shey Mureed said he would never refuse anything if asked for by ministrels on Thursday mornings. Sometime later Mir Chaakar sent a band of ministrels to Mureed's house on a Thursday morning, who played their instruments, sang and danced. Mureed asked them what he could offer them. They said they wanted that he should forego Haani, his fiancé, and cancel the engagement. Mureed, to keep his vow, had to concede the request. Mir Chaakar afterwards, married Haani. Mureed repented much and gave up normal life and became a derwesh. Haani continued to love him. The poet narrates what Haani wanted to offer to the person who could bring news of Mureed:
Shey he kas thara haala danth
Mesthaagi daey thou chihe?
Gushthe goun dile armaana:
Durraane dian jadenaan,
Kundigaan kawaant bahahenaan,
Ponze pullukk o graanzigaan,
Dasthe sangahaan Sibi ay,
Paade maarsarien paadinkaan,
Bachch goun gwanzaga shaagina,
Kull goun si hazaari ganjaan,
Chaakar goun selah o sanjaan,
Hanga sar mani kurbaaninth.

member of the tribe. He took part in discussions in Diwaan which was open to everyone, at the house of the Sardar or the elder. Sometimes, there was a separate place, Diwaanjaah, for such gatherings. Social, political and economic problems concerning the tribe were debated in these assemblies. Diwaan literally means gathering or assembly.

Diwaan in its formal nature was to be participated in by the elders and selected personalities. In all informal get-togethers, everybody felt his presence. This spirit had made the Baloch into a close-knit tribal structure based on mutual benefit and loss.

The house of the leader or *Diwaanjaah* was the place where history, legends, ballads, drama, [24] lyrics and tales of love were told and sung. Everyone wished that he could exert himself and attract others by his knowledge and manners during such discussions. Mothers in their lullaby were desirous that their sons, when grown up, should show sagacity and create fame in Balochi Diwaan. [25]

Codes

Another cultural feature was the codes adopted by each tribe to communicate news or situations concerning tribal security or other important matters. It was equivalent to the modern cipher system of national states. Being an important and responsible member of the tribe, if anyone saw or guessed something important was to occur, he would take steps to convey the news to others. He would resort to codes or signals if there was no other way, such as drawing some sign on the highways, near a tribal well, on a stone, or setting fire at some conspicuous places, etc. Another method was to give apparently a meaningless call in a particular manner. Waving of flags was also common. When such signs were seen or noises heard by persons

---

24 There are instances that bards narrated stories and events of battles in front of the elders, and sometimes acted in a dramatic manner while describing the events and war personalities. This could be called a sort of undeveloped and rudimentary form of stage drame in Balochi literature.

25 Bachcharaa badin hele goun,
Dema pa gulaab shudieth,
Sheeri gardena mesk o aap,
Rocha goun malik diwaanenth,
Shap goun dramgwaren kaadaanenth,

belonging to the same tribe, they would easily decode those and took not only precautions but immediately informed the Sardar or others in the manner suitable under the circumstances.

Bijjaar

Baloch society was based on the principle of mutual benefit and loss. Hand of cooperation was extended to persons who were needy. One could ask for financial help from anyone. Subscriptions were raised on all important occasions and ceremonies, on marriage, death or any calamity or any event requiring expenditures which may be beyond the capacity of the individual to pay. If a person wanted to construct a new house, an embankment on his land, or if he was faced with some circumstances beyond comprehension requiring expenditure or if his flocks were lost through a general epidemic: or crops by flood, in such eventualities he asked for *bijjaar*, which was always forthcoming. The contribution was entirely voluntary. No amount was fixed for that contribution which could be in cash or in kind. This was, however, regarded as a debt of honor. Similar contribution and usually more than the original value would have been paid to the person who had already paid and the occasion had arrived for him to ask for help. It was not necessary for the needy person to go personally to everybody and ask for help on ceremonial occasions such as marriage. He could depute someone for the collection of subscription on his behalf. Occasionally, the Sardar also asked for *bijjaar* for a needy tribesman.

There were also various other systems of helping or extending assistance to fellow tribesmen. They were termed as *chankuk, a* contribution in food grain after each harvest: *nikaan*, assistance to the neighbor in kind: and *baanji* which was a help in prepared food to the neighbor. If someone died in a family, there was no cooking, *aasrok*, for at least three days in that house. The neighbors would supply prepared foodstuffs for the family during these days.

The system of *bijjaar* has taken many definite shapes and names in the recent past. The Sardars and Chiefs also got contributions under this system: so also the headmen revoked this custom to get bijjaar but never paid back. It appears that in the early ages, the tribesmen would always volunteer to offer a subscription to meet the expenses of the Sardar. This practice was institutionalized and the Sardar was helped after every harvest. However, after the disintegration of Baloch tribal structure in the 19th century, the Sardars began to demand contributions even beyond the capacity of the individual to pay. There are instances when the Sardars extracted *bijjaar* by force.

Hawaachk

Hawaachk was the physical labor contributed towards a person's requirements. Work in plowing someone's fields or reaping of crops: work to build a house for a neighbor, or any other kind of physical labor for others came under the general definition of *hawaachk*. This was the dignified way of assisting another by offering personal services. As there was no hired labor in the tribal society, *hawaachk* fulfilled a pressing need.

Crimes and Punishments

An offense against the individual such as theft or robbery was a corporate offense against the entire tribe. Any contravention was punished according to the nature of the crime committed. But if the offense was committed outside the tribe, it was considered an offense against that tribe. The individual acts consequently would become the responsibility of the tribe concerned. His family and the entire people suffered. The opposing tribesmen could revenge the guilt in an appropriate manner; not necessarily against that particular individual but against any person belonging to the tribe of the offender.

The sentence for a misdemeanor was the payment of appropriate fine or compensating the loss of property in case of theft or robbery. Sometimes, robbery was also punished with death. Punishment of corporate crime was outlawry of the person that is disowning the individual, outcasting and declaring him isolated from the tribe. This was one of the major punishments and rarely awarded. In that case, he was also banished from the area.

There is the least evidence of awarding punishment of *dorekashshag* (tearing to pieces by pulling the accused in opposite directions by two horses); *Paahao* (hanging), which was awarded to traitors and the enemy agents. These forms of punishment nevertheless were clearly a later addition and not the original Baloch practices. Beheading was the common mode of inflicting the sentence. There is, however, no evidence of any permanent hangman among the Baloch for the purpose of executing criminals. In Kalat State, there was no permanent post of a hangman. The death sentence, however, was always awarded in public.

There is no evidence of punishment of death by drowning, throwing from rock, burning or burying alive,[26] pouring molten lead on the criminal, starvation in the dungeons tearing to dearth by red hot pincers, cutting asunder and stoning to death or the practice of blinding and maiming. The Baloch thought it more honorable to be beheaded than hanged. Other modes of capital punishment were thought to be insulting.

In cases of murder, the relative of the deceased had the inalienable right to claim blood for blood; and this claim had the tribal code of conduct, the deceased family and had the entire tribal strength. The murderer could be forgiven only by the nearest kin. Among a few tribes, blood compensation was given by the offender or his family. Relatives of the offender had to accept the punishment and were obliged to agree to the award sanctioned by elders if no settlement was reached. Extreme torture or dishonoring was against the tribal norm. However, torture to low castes involving in serious crimes was sometimes perpetrated.

The only crime which could invoke the death penalty or banishment besides treason was adultery. Sometimes mere suspicion of unfaithfulness by the wife was sufficient to put her to death. The man would also get the same punishment. But among some tribes who were alleged to be inferior in caste, the adulterous women were divorced and the adulterer was obliged to marry her. In the case of adultery, there was no need for the aggrieved husband to resort to any tribal council to get a decision. He himself inflicted the sentence. The unmarried women or widows got punishment from their near relatives.

---

26 Romans inflicted death penalty by drowning at sea, precipitating from Tarpeian rock, burying alive and beating to death. Superstitious forms of punishment, i.e throwing the criminal into water in a sack which also contained a dog, a cock, a viper and an ape was also of Roman origin which existed up to Middle Ages in many countries. Jews also employed extreme forms of punishment against the conquered peopless of Palestine in Biblical times.

A very peculiar cultural trait was that even the criminal or offender if apprehended would never tell a lie even in the face of instant punishment. This was against his sense of honor and pride. He was always truthful. This made torture to extract information or confession of guilt quite unnecessary.

Among the ancient Baloch, like other Aryan groups trial by ordeal was perhaps in vogue. The culprit had to prove his innocence by walking through the fire or putting his hands on a hot rod. In Balochi folk stories there are numerous instances when the innocence of the offender had to be proved by putting his hands on the hot stone, *thaapag*. This practice was perhaps discarded in the later periods.

In most cultures, any child of less than 14 years of age was usually considered incapable of guilt on the ground that he or she was too young to differentiate between right and wrong. The practice was completely reversed among the Baloch. The Baloch child had a penetrating since regarding his enemies and friends. Old blood accounts sometimes were settled by persons of less than 14 years. A Baloch child took part in battles. Therefore, the case of guilt or criminal responsibility for the minor was always judged according to circumstance and merit of the case. The members of the family of the minor would have to bear the responsibility of his guilt if the crime was provoked by them.

The home of a Baloch Sardar or elder was a safe refuge and place of protection for all the offenders of law until the decision of the dispute through the *council of elders* or *meid*.

Meid

Meid was a unique social phenomenon. It had a prime place in the adjudication of disputes between individuals and groups. There was a difference between *meid* and *jirga* which had a separate sphere and meaning. The meid was a voluntary effort by responsible Individuals to solve the disputes, while jirga replaced the council of elders and became an institutionalized form of the tribal structure since the occupation of Balochistan in the mid 19th century.

While deciding the cases of murder, the *jirga* particularly had no power because the aggrieved party seldom presented its case to it. He always wanted compensation in blood only. The blood compensation had no time bar. The spirit of revenge persisted and remained smart for two hundred years like a young deer of tender age as the saying goes: *Bier Balochaani than dosad saala, lassaen aahuge dodanthaanen!* However, the *jirga* may sometimes take the shape of *meid* and could be requested by the offender side to intervene to solve the dispute. The aggrieved party could be contacted and requested to agree to *meid* in accordance with tradition. Generally, they conceded. Then the jirga which may include many tribal elders and social personalities would go to the house of the victim and accept without any reservation the guilt of the offender and offer an unconditional apology on behalf of the person and ask formally the forgiveness and magnanimity of the host. The aggrieved family then declares its forgiveness and the matter would end there. The *meid* could not be taken to the house of the victim without the prior consent of the head of the family or clan in cases of the great injustice or inhuman cruelty. Simple murder cases of sudden nature provoked by the deceased were, however, the easiest to be solved through *meid*.

Members or persons who constituted *meid* were not elected or had any authority save the moral pressure they could exert. The elders usually sent feelers to the parties for the solution of the dispute through a *meid* and someone acted as a conciliatory go-between.

In tribal philosophy, the individual was of supreme importance and matters concerning him could be tackled only through his consent. Surprisingly, even the entire tribe could not force him to agree to a decision regarding any dispute in which he was a party. Secondly, the right to revenge or agree to compensation for the loss he suffered was the inalienable right exercised by him and not by any person or group of persons on his behalf. Thirdly, he always wanted to make the culprit accountable for his wrong; and once he admitted his guilt, it would be honorable for him to forgive if requested. Such an act was always considered appropriate and behoving a Baloch. Fourthly, the proud Baloch could not refuse the requests of persons who were his guest of honor and that once in the house they could not be treated as hostiles.

Apart from the *meid*, he would usually forgive the culprit if he personally entered the house premises of the aggrieved family, accepted his guilt and requested the magnanimity and forgiveness of the victim's relatives. This was called *loge putherag*. After this act of the person, he was generally forgiven and the feud ended there.

Meid was resorted to in individual disputes as well as tribal feuds. In the former case, elders of the clans or sub-clans would go as meid while in the later, various tribal heads constituted the meid. Once the aggrieved party consented and received the guests, he was honor bound to accept the pleading of the *meid* and resolve the dispute. If he did not agree it would be an insult to all the persons who acted as *meid* and they would become a party to the dispute and practically took the side of the opposite party in any active contest between them in future.

For all practical purposes, *meid* was more useful and commonly resorted to than the *jirga. Jirga* could deal with a case when it was submitted for arbitration by the parties in dispute and agreed to accept the decision. Since the Baloch believed in his own action in revenging blood feuds or compensating any wrong perpetrated, he seldom submitted his case for arbitration to *jirga*.

Caste system

The caste system prevailing among the Baloch had a contrasting parallel with the Indian caste system which was based on religious beliefs.[27] Among the Baloch, it had no religious overtures. Historically, certain peoples of an indigenous origin subjugated by the Baloch after their migration to these areas were regarded as their social inferiors.[28]

---

27   The Indian caste system developed out of a multi racial society. The Aryans might have contributed toward the system because of their dislike of dark-skinned Indians whom they regarded as their inferiors. Religious sanctity in Indian caste system slowly took firm roots afterward. A hymn of Rig Veda, provides a somewhat mystical origin of the caste:
When the gods made a sacrifice with the man as their victim.
When they divided the man into how many parts did they divide him?
What was his mouth, what were his arms, what were his thighs and his feet called?
The Brahman was his mouth, of his arms were made the warrior.
His thighs became the Vaishya, of his feet the Shudra was born.
With sacrifice, the gods sacrificed to sacrified. These were the first of the sacred laws.
These mighty beings reached the sky, where are the eternal spirits, the gods.
(Quoted by Romila Thapar, Op Cit p.39-40)

28   Among the indigenous peoples, Jat, Darzaadag, Jadgaal, Laangao, and Lodi were not awarded equal social status until recently while slaves and their descendants, Nakeeb, were regarded low-castes.

A Baloch did not mix up with those people because he feared that he might lose his racial identity and purity of blood. It appears that the distinction was based mostly on color also. The local people were usually dark skinned, while the Baloch were of fairer complexion. They had no role to play in political and military endeavors of "the master race" and were employed to perform certain duties including the cultivation of lands and other miscellaneous works beneficial to all. The Baloch never allowed inter-marriages with these people who nevertheless were aligned with one Baloch tribe or the other and even participated in their wars.

Among the Baloch themselves, there was complete social equality. Every person had equal rights and privileges and recognized social status. All were warriors and equally took part in the battle. No one, not even the tribal chief, had more rights than the ordinary Baloch. No one could boast a superior status. The Baloch was egoistic and extremely conscious of his exalted position. Beebagr's boasting that *Kay mani gahgeerin sara guddieth (Who can cut my majestic head?)* could be appreciated only through the Baloch sense of pride. Shey Mureed challenged Mir Chaakar saying that he did not enjoy any superior position except being the tribal Chief. Haibithaan refused to give back Mir Chaakar's bull-camel to keep his vow. On each and every occasion, a Baloch was an equal partner. Though he had greatest regards for the Chief, he never compromised his identity and freedom to act independently. There was no class of aristocracy or warrior distinguished from the ordinary Baloch nor was there any class of clergymen who could have any marked influence on political and military matters.

As the Baloch considered all other professions except warfare below his masterly status, there might have developed hereditary professions among non-Baloch tribes. While he chose himself the task of warfare which was always regarded as a noble pursuit, his allied indigenous tribes engaged in other fields of tribal endeavor. However, Baloch considered cattle rearing also an honorable pursuit. Agriculture as a profession came in vogue at a much later stage. Surprisingly, he still does not have any skill in trade and commerce.

It is, however difficult to assert as to who the pure Baloch tribes are now. There has been a considerable mingling of various peoples through the centuries. The Baloch kept concubines and slave girls and their offshoots slowly came to be recognized as Baloch. The chiefs took girls from allied tribes as did the war heroes, commanders, and other nobles. Therefore, though the racial purity has now become doubtful in many cases, the Baloch still has the greatest considerations for racial purity and status. He never gives his woman to a racially inferior man whatever may be his economic position.[29]

Slavery

In a historical context, individuals were reduced to slavery when they were captured in battles, sold for punishing an offense, or non-payment of debts or sometimes sold by parents. Slavery was mentioned as an institution in Sumer. The Sumerian word for slavery literally means 'a woman from a foreign land'. However, the Greeks explained the institution of slavery as governed on the intellectual inferiority of certain races. Romans justified it from an imaginary agreement between the victor and the vanquished in which the later impliedly agree to a servile dependency. For moral justification, it appears that slavery must have some religious sanctions.

Slavery came in the Baloch social life after their movement from the Caspian region and dominating the areas which now constitutes Balochistan. They kept local people as servile dependents. The institution received a boost in the second half of the first millennium of the Christian era. Not only conquering Arab princes brought a considerable number of slaves but later on Arab traders brought Negros from East African seaports and sailed them across the Indian ocean to Muscat and Oman and then to southern Balochistan. Apart from buying slaves, the Baloch obtain them after their periodic raids into enemy territory. But no Baloch was reduced to slavery after their defeat in the battle. Even in the time of victory, they never ill-treated their vanquished brethren. All the slaves belonged either to the indigenous population or people of African descent brought into Balochistan by way of trade and commerce or by the conquering Arab armies. There were also slaves of Maratha and Hazara origin.

Before its abolition in the 19th century by the British, slavery was very general throughout Balochistan. Every noble family possessed a

---

29 Jadgaals are supposed to be Dravidians. They were among the original inhabitants of Kirman, Sistan and Makkuran before the Baloch arrived in these areas.

number of male or female slaves whose status was one of degradation. They were employed in labor; the kind, degree and the time were to be determined by the master. All legal, economic and social right of the slaves were to be exercised by the owner. Persons deputed by the master had the same authority over the slaves which the original owner had. They were considered as personal belongings and could be sold and gifted to any person. A slave did not have the means to free himself. He was hereditary and perpetual. Female slaves were kept as concubines and servants. The owner did not forego the right of sexual access even after the slave woman was married to a slave man. It was, however, considered a disgrace for a Baloch to free a slave on payment. He could get his liberty if he or she performed some extraordinary service for his master. Sometimes slaves were freed when requested by him or her at the time of the master's death.

The Baloch were more human in treating their slaves as compared to most other peoples. They disapproved inhuman torture to their slaves. A slave in a bad condition or hungry or ill-dressed was considered to be an insult for his owner. Slaves born in the house of the owner were usually better treated than those newly acquired. Most slaved were assigned important tasks by their masters, and they came to acquire a position of trust and confidence. Various Khans of Kalat treated the slaves well and even put them on important governmental jobs. Shahgasi Noor Mahmad, Daroga Gul Mahmad, and Rahimdad were put on important governmental positions.

The Domb

Lodi or domb are believed to be among thousands of entertainers brought from India by Sassanid Emperor Bahram Gor and distributed among various nations and tribes of his empire. The *domb* or *Lodi* had become an institution and had a recognized place in society. He acted as a messenger in many important matters. In social events, he was ahead of all. He generally made all the arrangements during marriage ceremonies including musical concerts and feasting the guests. He also made arrangements on a variety of other ceremonies from birth to death. Later, some of the *dombs* also became professional workers. Their manual labor included making instruments or tools for agricultural use. He, however, got contributions on various ceremonial occasions and times of harvests to meet his expenses. He had certain privileges. He was never harmed in time of war or peace.

Status and responsibilities of a woman

In the Baloch patriarchal set-up, a woman was generally regarded to be incapable of shouldering the onerous responsibilities as an active member in wars. For this, apparently, she did not enjoy that much power and prestige. Her position nevertheless had been one of respect and love, sharing to a great extent the man's burden in many ways. Although women's position was generally considered as one of subservience, the Baloch considered a woman a full partner in all social endeavors and accorded her a position of trust and favor.[30] She had to perform many obligations as a member of the family and as a mother. In the absence of close male members, the woman did enjoy the patriarchal powers as the guardian of the family and property. She, therefore, had recognized rights and privileges. She was not only to do the household work but also take part in manly occupations such as grooming of horses, grazing of flocks and assisting in cultivation. Apart from the routine work, she made a very different variety of embroidery. Her shirts were embroidered with handwork of very beautiful and artistic nature. Embroidery was also done on man's shirts and other articles. Cotton yarn was also spun by the women for use by men in the weaving of clothes.

The woman was always taken into confidence in a time of grave emergency. While organizing war, their counsels were also taken into consideration because they had to take part in war efforts and fulfill certain obligations. They generally did not take part in the battles alongside men but the tribal wars were almost total in their character: and every person had to participate, if required, in the battle. Women, however, usually provided medical and civil assistance to the wounded.

In spite of the fact that the women were active participants in the war efforts, they were always spared. The Baloch women after a victory in an intertribal war were never enslaved. On the contrary, if

---

30 In some societies women had no rights. They were purchased, and marriage was on payment of bride price. In Arab and other Semitic societies, a wife could have been lent to a guest as a mark of hospitality or handed over to a friend for sexual intimacy when the husband went on a journey.

women intervened in the battle, the war was stopped and negotiations began for settlement of the dispute. The killing of a woman was considered an act of cowardice. It was a matter of honor that women were treated well and never harmed.

There are some very famous women in Baloch political history that exercised tremendous influence and are known for their sagacity and wisdom. The Mother of Mir Naseer Khan, Bibi Mariam gave audiences to the Sardars and has political discussions with them in the absence of her son. She also accompanied the Khan during battles, and her counsels in war matters were respected. Bibi Ganjaan, mother of Khudadaad Khan used to give political advice to the Khan and took part in the administration and decision making of the Khanate. Bibi Baanadi, the sister of Mir Chaakar took part in the Battle of Panipat (1556-A.D) against the Suris in support of Emperor Humayun. According to Baloch traditions, she commanded a section of Baloch troops. (There is no historical evidence of any Baloch army under the command of Bibi Baanadi in the battle of Panipat; this is mentioned in one of the classical poems appears to have no substance). On one occasion when the Baloch Lashkar appeared to be withdrawing from the battlefield, she boldly came forward, taunted and reminded the Baloch that a true Baloch never leaves the battlefield for fear of death. It is said that Baloch Lashkar remained in the battlefield, withstanding the severe attacks against considerable losses, and contributed a great deal in the final victory. The sister of Mir Ahmad Khan I (1666-1696 A.D) Mai Beebu, was killed fighting in the fifteenth battle against the Barozais of Sibi. Gohar Maaheri showed great acumen by not telling Mir Chaakar, the chief of Rind tribe the fact regarding the killing of her camels by Lashaari youth because she rightly feared hostilities between Rind and Lashaar, which she prudently wanted to avoid. According to traditions, Mir Chaakar visited Gohar in her settlement. He saw the she-camels of Gohar whose udders were full of milk which was coming out from the teats of the animals. Mir Chaakar guessed something wrong and asked Gohar what the matter was. She did not tell the truth. However, Gohar's shepherd narrated the entire story of the killing of the baby-camels by Lashaar. On this grave provocation, Mir Chaakar declared war upon Lashaar.

There had been no system of *parda or* segregation of sexes. To fulfill their social responsibilities, women always mixed up with menfolk. However, in recent history, segregation was practiced among middle classes and a few ruling families mostly through alien influences.

The Baloch gave a substantial share to women in the property. In the contemporary Baloch society, except for some tribes in central Balochistan, a woman gets her share in the property and inherits from her husband as well as from blood relatives but the share is not equal to the man of the family.

Unlike ancient practices which subordinated a woman to her blood relations, the Baloch always subordinated her to her husband. Her social rights rested not with her blood relations but with her husband. The husband was responsible for her every action. If she committed a crime, the prime burden rested on the husband: but her other kin would also offer assistance or bear the brunt of any ill-fame she might have brought. Her relatives would always be a party if injustice was done to her. If she was divorced without any socially acceptable reason, her people would consider it a great insult and would take appropriate revenge.

A woman was expected to be extremely faithful. Punishment of unfaithfulness was not less than death. The faithfulness of a wife was of prime importance. Among some of the Brahui speaking tribes, it was generally an accepted principle that virginity of the bride was to be tested by displaying to close relations the blood-stained clothes after the first intercourse between husband and wife as a testimonial of her virginity. If she did not prove to be a virgin, she met the fate of an adulterous woman. But the punishment was given by the relative of women and not by the husband because the alleged crime was committed before she was married. In that eventuality, the husband immediately declared a divorce and sent the girl to her relatives who would kill her. The entire property or *labb* that is given to the bride by the husband and expenses incurred by him would be restored and paid back. The genesis of this practice is not known, but it is clear that it was not an original Baloch custom; it must have come through foreign influences. After committing an act of adultery, or *Siahkaari*, if the women managed to escape instant punishment and reached the house of a Sardar or any elder, then she was saved. The husband would divorce her and get some compensation from her or from her family. But the husband retained the right to retaliate against the adulterous man, the *Siahkaar*. The relative of a woman may also retaliate against the adulterous person responsible for bringing ill fame for them.

The Baloch was very cautious in selecting his wife because only a noble, respectable and bounteous lady could bear glorious sons. Sons who could earn fame for themselves and their forefathers could never be born to mediocre women. Similarly, according to the Baloch social beliefs, gracious daughters could not be born by ordinary men.[31] While selecting a wife he had great consideration for his match to be of equal racial standing. Marriage with the low castes was always considered degrading. The wife must be hospitable, responsible and beautiful. Moreover, she must have womanly qualities of modesty, faithfulness, and devotion. Young virgin ladies seldom made up their face or wore red clothes. Modesty and shyness were considered good for them. The beauty criteria were that she should have black and large eyes, small white teeth, thin lips, broad and open face; fair color, thin and high nose, tiny feet, thin and long fingers, a long neck, medium height, and long black hair. The Baloch considered an egg-shaped head for a woman (also for a man) very ugly. It should be round. For this, they would make a lot of efforts for shaping the head of the child according to their wishes.

The Baloch lady had the onerous responsibility to teach her son the principles of their great forefathers and bring him up as a brave and enterprising youth. She should teach him how glorious it is to fight and to be killed in the battlefield, and how shameful it would be not only for him but for the entire family and tribe to run away from the battlefield. Therefore the position of a mother who bore great children was unique. Her position was further exalted when she became the mother of a son who was to be reared to shoulder the future responsibilities of the family, keeping the enemies at bay and establishing the bonds of love with friends. Her daughter would have similar responsibilities. She sings lullabies expecting her to be a lady of highest qualities, being hospitable and faithful. In her lullabies, she praises her daughter for womanly qualities. She imagines that a noble would request her to grant him the hands of her beautiful and graceful daughter in marriage. But for being accepted as a son-in-law and in order to fulfill the wishes of the mother and her daughter, the would-be son-in-law would suffer a lot:

---

31 Do daanki mathaan hassadi bachch nabanth,
  Chiller o legaarin pithaan graan naazen jenikk.

"He would woo her for a year, wearing out four pairs of shoes in the process. Six months would pass in the negotiations for the confirmation of betrothal, habarsindi. For labb, he would offer countless money, besides a large quantity of gold. He would offer landed property. He would give a score of buffaloes from Dewal; three hundred camels of the best breed; three hundred pairs of embroidered clothes and three hundred frizzled haired slave girls". [32]

She thinks her daughter would be a lady of high standing in the community. Like a lady lord, she would receive the guests. When her brother comes with his close comrades and stays with her as a guest, she would order slaying of buffaloes for dinner and sheep for lunch. [33] She praises her for her beauty, hospitality and wealth.

---

32 Kad bieth o kujaam baandaanth beith,
Mirchuke mani zaamaath bieth,
Juthke mochadi shinginith,
Say juthke aahini kosh dirrieth,
Saale man raho ahaan bieth,
Shash maaha habarsindi bieth,
Zarra chu jawa johaan kanth,
Suhra chu kuroche hosha,
Machche cha Khurasan biyareth,
Punse yakdaren thankaahe,
Lutte nezahanth Thurkaani,
Machchaan granbaren Dishthaari
Hoshaan be hesaaba kaarieth,
Luttani sarish kaththaarieth
Hoshe zarrint o hoshe suhr,
Hoshe yakdaren murwaarid.
(Bale) raazeeg nabith pa aishaan,
Raazeeg nabieth laale maath
Loti Diwali gaameshaan,
Say sad chinukanth pur nakshin,
Say sad daachianth nok gwamsin,
Say sad moledanth pilpil put,
Drustan pa gule labbaan danth,

33 Bachchi shah janani bibi,
Chu pishinnin janaan paadketh,
Gwank janth molidaan karegaan,
Shunahith wathi mehmanaan,
Brathia Khuda zuth biyarieth,

84

Lulla, lulla lullaby,
Lulla, Moon face, Lullaby.
Thou art Queen among thy sisters,
Like the Moon mid starry clusters.
Lulla, lulla lullaby,
Lulla, Moon face, Lullaby.
My lady's tent is high and wide,
And thirty paces long besides,
It heads the camp, and from after
Guests come from Bhaag and Kandahar.
Lulla, lulla lullaby,
Lulla, Moon face, Lullaby.
Her lord owns flock and herds that thrive,
The proud lord of Kech or Chief of the tribe,
Three weary years he comes to woo,
Aye, thrice he wears out either shoe,
Close-packed as dates his gifts are stored,
Like barley stacks his golden hoard
Lulla, lulla lullaby,
Lulla, Moon face, Lullaby. [34]

The mother was perhaps the most important tutor for her son and daughter, especially on matters of traditional values and morality.

Polygamy

It appears that the Baloch practiced polygamy, and there was no bar on the number of wives. It was believed to be a mark of honor and resourcefulness. Not necessarily every person married more that one wife; but the man who could pay *labb* (bride-price) and marriage expenses, and is in a position to maintain them, usually married more than one wife. Tribal sardars married for a political reason as well. The well-to-do had concubines besides their wives.

Kaith (wati) haddiay mehmaan bieth.
Shap shaama kushith gaameshaan,
Nemrocha nazankin meshaan

34 Denys Bray, The life History of a Brahui, (first published London: royal Asiatic Society, 1913) Reprint in Pakistan: Royal Book company, Karachi 1977, p.21-22

If we analyze the tribal structure we will find that polygamy was not solely for sex purposes. Among many ancient peoples, the sex element was not the only factor for polygamy, which was also true of the Baloch. A plurality of wives increased the probability of offspring who were considered assets and were never repudiated nor are there any traces of infanticide, as was the custom in many middle eastern peoples. Children were economic incentives and always desired by both men and women. A man's supply of labor increased substantially by his marrying more wives and bearing more children. In a tribal structure where there was no hired labor, this must have been an important consideration. Another important factor for polygamy had been the idea to absorb the surplus women: widows or virgins. Engaged in a constant struggle, women were always numerous compared to men because the latter were killed in battles in large numbers.

The plurality of wives was a mark of distinction. The sister in her lullaby to her baby-brother wished him to marry at least seven ladies. She wanted a promising tomorrow when her brother will be a young man and be the husband of seven beautiful wives.[35]

The Baloch seldom married outside his clan or tribe. Cousins and close relatives were preferred. There was great regard for blood relatives because they were considered more trustworthy and loyal.

The woman whose husband died or was killed on the battlefield was allowed to remarry. But the preference was given to the relatives of the husband in giving the hands of the widow in a second marriage because it was always pinching for the entire family that the wife of their brother or cousin should become the wife of another person not related to them. In cases of the remarriage of a widow, there was to be no ceremony. Remarriage was affected in a very simple and austere manner as a mark of respect to the deceased. Even if she married outside her ex-husband's family, the marriage ceremonies would be quite simple.

The usual marriages were celebrated with a variety of festivities including music and dances; but if a widower wanted to remarry the

---

35   Kad bieth o kujaam bandaath bieth,
     Brathi markabaan swari bieth,
     Brathi hapth jane jodi bieth,
     Leelo leel kanith brathia,
     Brath (o) sad muraadin laala.

ceremony would have been simple for the man. However, the woman's side would arrange the full ceremonies if she was a virgin.

Divorce

Divorce was regarded as an insult.[36] It was inconceivable that a lady who once was the wife of a gentleman may marry another person. In social ethos, it was always remembered with bad connotation for ex-husband and also for the new one. The divorcee was called *Najan*, ex-wife of so and so even after many years of divorce and remarriage. Perhaps a very strong reason for social disapproval of divorce and remarriage of a woman had its rationale from social problems which followed. The children who would be with her mother at the time of infancy were again an insult to his sense of pride that sons or daughters of an honorable person may remain in the house of a man who had married his ex-wife.

Barrenness or being a *sant*, for the women, was perhaps the most unfortunate event in her life. The blame was equally laid on man, but not so often. Barrenness on the part of women could result in a second marriage by the husband or, in rare cases, lead to a separation.

If a woman was divorced for her own fault, the husband would claim the labb or bride gifts he had given to her. But if the marriage was dissolved for any other reason he would forego the *labb*. There are instances when separation became necessary. The impotence of man or barrenness of wife could be the major factors. There appear to be no other reasons which invoked a divorce. Divorce among the low-castes was, however, frequent on even petty matters of dispute. No formal ceremony was required for the annulment of marriage which was quite simple. But later under Arabian religious influences, throwing

---

36 Divorce was not uncommon because of any religious sanctity of marriage but because it was socially disapproved. In Christianity divorce is not allowed because the Catholic Church considers marriage as a sacrament. In other civilizations, however, divorce for man and woman had been easy. The Mosaic law allowed a husband to give a bill of divorcement; Chinese law allowed divorce provided the property which the wife brought with her marriage was restored. Among the Baloch, the property had to be restored in case the divorce was demanded by wife. Similarly, the wife was to be compensated if she was divorced by the husband without any socially acceptable reason.

three coins or objects towards the women, whether present or not, and declaring from that time that the woman would not be his wife, would be enough to legalize the divorce.

In the case of unfaithfulness, the punishment was death. Eloping with a married woman was usually unknown. Its punishment was also death. But if the woman could escape instant death and manage to reach the house of the Sardar or village elder after alleged adultery, then the dispute was resolved after negotiation which would result in a divorce. But it did not mean that the Sardar could become partial or take the woman's side. As the woman came under his protection (the adulterous person would not be protected by anybody as a matter of principle) he would not allow any harm to come to her. She would not be handed over to her relatives till the decision of the dispute, because that most probably cause a feud between the husband and the relatives of the woman or provoking the murder of the woman by her relatives. In such cases, the husband was compensated and the woman was allowed to marry her adulterous lover because generally, nobody else would be willing to marry such a woman. Surprisingly, the man who caused the entire affair could not be compelled to marry the woman because he may resort to ethical standards and refuse to marry the woman who had betrayed her previous husband. As for man, his sexual adventures were generally hailed with approval as a mark of courage and manliness, while the wife's conduct was utterly condemned with extreme punishment.

It was not the duty of the husband alone to give the woman punishment for adultery. The husband and her own family both would condemn her to death whoever would get the chance first or saw her on the occasion or strongly suspected such an act on her part. The right of the husband to retaliate against his ex-wife's lover did not end even after the divorce was formalized. Such a person mostly to avoid reprisal would leave that area and settle somewhere else so that the husband may not harm him. If the woman was refused marriage by her lover she was given in marriage to some stranger or to a person unaware of the entire episode. If a man and a woman were taken in adultery and killed, there would be no usual ceremonies for their burials. Sometimes they were taken in a most contemptuous manner and interred in a common grave.

Concubinage

Keeping concubines was perhaps one of the most ancient practices among the Baloch. Concubinage, (*sureath*) became a regular phenomenon in a later stage in history when, as conquering tribes, the Baloch kept women as concubines. In the beginning, probably it was restricted at first instance to the Chiefs and war heroes or those who showed exemplary valor in the battle. Later in the Muslim era, it became a regular feature, and Muslim generals and rulers kept concubines and dancing girls. The Arab and Central Asian tradition of homosexuality also crept and persisted in the Baloch society to some extent. However, the Arab practice of keeping handsome pages with them in the confines of their *harems* did not creep into Baloch society. The Baloch had never kept a Baloch woman as a concubine. They always were from the low-caste or from amongst the slaves.

Prostitution was practically unknown. The venal love had no place. Lover relationship was completely voluntary. A woman had to be won through courageous acts of a promising man of high character. Prostitution and rape were hated. The Baloch women even in love could hardly transgress the social limits. She could not elope with the lover nor even contemplate it because that would bring ill-fame to her family, father and glorious brother. Gifts were exchanged between the lovers as symbols of their affection for each other.

Inheritance

It was generally the eldest son who took up the administration and responsibility of the family at the death of his father. But he was not the only shareholder in his father's property. Other sons and daughters also, had the right to inherit. It appears that the ancient Baloch gave a little share to the daughter from her father's possessions; the bulk would go to the sons who must have inherited proportionately. The eldest son got *'Mirwandi'* that was an extra share apart from the normal share he was entitled to. It was not legally binding but was granted as a mark of courtesy. As regards the wife, she had most possibly received a reasonable share.

It is probable that the son had acquired a vested right in father's property after his death. But as long as the father was living he had considerable authority. Usually, the father gave away a portion of his wealth, according to the general law, to the sons who attained maturity. The parents in certain cases might have retained the nominal property. As regard daughters, they shared property after their father's death. There are also instances when she always got a few essential articles at the time of her marriage and no other demands were put on father's property afterward. The Khan of Kalat, Mir Naseer Khan's seven daughters were allowed no share in the property beyond presents and gifts consisting of dresses and jewelry at the time of their marriages.

It appears that the will by no means could disinherit a son from his father's belongings. The deceased's will was however accorded due recognition and respect on matters of tribal and social importance, but it had no strong impact especially when it was against the general principles of tribal society. An old Balochi saying means the deceased's message to the surviving members of his family is an exercise in futility because the heir acts in whatever manner he wishes (*Murdag kulah kanth zindaga, bale Zindag hama kanth wathi dil*).

The father's close relatives had perhaps a share in the property because they had to shoulder certain responsibilities in connection with their deceased relative's children and the widow who had to marry some kinsman of her husband. Therefore, it is probable that to maintain that link, relatives had some vested right in the assets in certain eventualities.

The sons had no share in the mother's personal articles such as utensils, clothing, and jewelry. They were equally distributed among the daughters. The father's personal belongings were shared by the sons. Sons and daughters of concubines had no share. Similarly, adopted children accorded no right to inherit; but there was no bar on the father to give a portion of the property to an adopted son. If a woman remarried against the consent of her deceased husband's relatives, she would get no share from the property of her ex-husband.

If a person was dead without a male or female heir, his wealth passed on to his close blood relatives. If he had no such living relatives, the property was given to the wife. After the father's death, his grandfather or brothers assumed the charge of guardianship. If he had no blood relations surviving, the wife and her relatives assumed those responsibilities until the sons' attained full age.

It may be pointed out that there was no private ownership of land by an individual. The entire cultivable lands and grazing fields were jointly owned by all tribesmen. The produce was equally distributed. Land ownership by the individual came during recent epochs especially after the occupation of Balochistan during which the pace of the disintegration of tribal structure got momentum.

Hospitality

The Baloch was hospitable. The guest was a mark of respect and held as almost sacred. Hospitality had a prime place in tribal ethos. Even the enemy, once entered in the house, would get the treatment of an honored guest. The guest in a village was visited by all elders and also the ladies, enquiring in the traditional way, of his well-being and that of his relatives and friends.

The well to do persons had a separate house or tent for the guests. If a stranger approached a village, the inmates present would receive him with all courtesy and serve him with all kinds of available food. If any male member was not present, it was the duty of females to receive the guest. He could stay for as many days as he liked. If he desired to leave he was given necessary articles according to the distance he wished to travel if he did not possess any for the remaining journey.

The Baloch were hospitable not only to common folk but to any person in distress. Bakhshu's hospitability and help to the fleeing Mughal Emperor Humayun is a glaring example. When he reached Multan on his way to Persia after his disastrous defeat at the hands of Sher Shah Suri, he was short of supplies. He also needed boats to cross the Indus. Bakhshu sent him about a hundred boats, loaded with grain. Humayun divided the corn among his men and used the boats for crossing the Indus.[37]

Malik Khatee's treatment to the unfortunate prince was another example of Baloch generosity even at the cost of earning the enmity of the powerful rulers of Kandahar. Humayun with a few men reached near a Baloch settlement in Chagai. He was approached by some thirty people and asked not to move on till the arrival of their Chief. The Emperor had to comply with their wish. The Baloch wife of Hasan Ali

---

37 Gul Badan Begum: Humayan Nama, Trans. Annetes Beverage (Pakistan Ed) Sang-e-Meel Publication, Lahore 1974, pp.147-148

the Chamberlain, who understood Balochi, heard these men saying that if they seized Humayun and took him to Mirza Askari, they would certainly be honored. This intended mischief was conveyed to the Emperor who ordered a strict watch around the camp. Late at night the chief Malik Khatee arrived and met the Emperor. He told Humayun that he has received a *Farman* from Mirza Askari to seize Humayun whenever he reached his area and take him to Kandahar. He had been warned of the consequence if he failed to comply with the orders. Malik Khatee, however, assured the Emperor that he had now no intention to capture him, and would rather sacrifice his life and that of his family for his sake.[38] According to traditions, Malik Khatee told the Mughal prince that he could easily arrest him and carry him to the Afghan ruler; but since he had arrived at his home and was his guest, he would now act according to Baloch customs. Malik Khatee escorted the Emperor safely to the border of Persia.

This hospitality had its rationale not only in tribal traditions but also due to geographical conditions of the vast land mass where the Baloch population was scattered. The distances were vast and means of communication limited. The traveler would have invariably suffered a lot of hardship without such hospitality. Without expecting such help it would have become rather impossible for any person to travel long distances. It appears that the Baloch also allowed any traveler to take a goat or sheep for the purpose of food from any herd which he might come across. This custom is, however no more in vogue.

Sanctity of home

The Baloch never violated the sanctity of home under any circumstances whatsoever. Even an offender who entered into the house premises of a Baloch was never pursued and apprehended because after entering the house, he was not only a guest but also a *Baahot* (a person given protection or refuge) and would be protected by all means. Sanctity of home was a universally accepted norm and based on reciprocity.

---

38   Ibid, pp.167-168.

Vows

Vows had a prime place in the Baloch society. When a Baloch made a vow or swore to do or not to do certain acts he would abide by that oath of honor. Sometimes such vows resulted in disastrous consequences. Mir Kambar took a vow not to return without recovering the persons and property taken away by Mir Mehraab. He preferred to be killed in the battle than come to a compromise which was offered during the fight. Mir Kambar was a chieftain. Mir Mehraab attacked the neighboring villages and plundered the property of some Hindu merchants. He also took away a few people to be exchanged for ransom. Mir Kambar, when informed, considered it an insult and decided to fight against the invading gang. Mir Kambar and his men encountered Mir Mehraab near Dizzik. Mir Kambar was killed during the fight. Graannaaz, a gracious lady made a vow not to be the wife of a coward, Lalla. Mir Chaakar swore to take revenge upon the Lashaar of the defeat of Nali and death of his close comrade, Meeraan and others who fell in the battle. He also swore that he would raise a small tower, *chidag*, on the ground out of the heads of Lashaar who would be killed in that battle and would sit upon those heads. He did what he had pledged to do.

The Baloch always swore by the head of his father or his sword, or he simply took his beard in his hands and said the words he intended to do or not to do. Mir Haibithaan made a vow not to return the camels of anyone who got mixed up with his herd. He refused to return Mir Chaakar's *saand*, a bull-camel, which got lost and joined those of his herd. It was a very agonizing situation not only for Haibithaan but also for the entire tribe when a noble from the tribe refused to return back the *saand* (The Bull-camel) of the mighty Sardar Mir Chaakar, just to keep his words. Ultimately, Mir Chaakar had to give in and declared that he would not demand his camel be recovered from Mir Haibithaan because he was aware that he would rather be killed than return the camel. Mir Jaado, a Rind nobleman, swore that he would kill anyone who laid hand on his beard in public and also he would kill anyone who may kill his friend, Huddeh. Subsequently, he even did not hesitate to kill his infant son who touched his beard. Jaado asked his nephew, Shaaho to kill Huddeh because he had touched his beard while crossing him on a horse-race. Then to keep his words he killed his nephew, Shaaho to avenge Huddeh's death. Shey Mureed made a vow that he would never refuse anything wanted by minstrels on a Thursday morning. He declared his intention publicly not to marry Haani to whom he was betrothed when requested by a band of minstrels sent purposefully by Mir Chaakar. He suffered a great deal mentally and had to leave the area for many years, became a Darwish but he kept his promise. One, Sumael, from Rind tribe, made a vow to marry a lady who may still be in the marriage of somebody. The ridiculous reason he gave was that normally everybody marries a virgin or a widow; he was determined to do something unprecedented. Subsequently, he married forcefully the wife of one Aadam in his absence. This became the cause of deep conflict and the open warfare between the two clans, resulting in the killing of many people.

Baahot

Another phenomenon was giving protection to a person who became a *Baahot*. *Baahot* was implicit or explicit; a neighbor was always regarded as under protection. Defending a Baahot was the prime duty of the Baloch who would never hesitate to take up arms to safeguard his life and property. Theoretically, every person could ask for this protection, which was never refused. However, proclaimed offenders usually were not accorded the privilege.

There are interesting instances in Baloch history when a Baloch took up arms to defend a *Baahot* and his property. The most peculiar was the animal *Baahot*, lizard, which resulted in the tribal conflict and the endless fight between Kalmathi and Bulfath tribes in the early eighteenth century. A few Kalmathi boys chased a lizard to kill it. The animal crept into the tent or *gidaan* of a neighboring Bulfathi, Oumar. Incidentally, there was no male member of the house present. Oumar's wife, Bibari, asked the boys not to kill the lizard as it had entered her house; and thus according to traditions was under her protection, as a *Baahot*. They did not listen to the lady's requests and entered the tent and killed the lizard. Bibari took a vow and told her husband that she would not remain her wife until he took the revenge of the lizard's death. Oumar ultimately decided to avenge and killed a Kalmathi. This developed into a tribal feud which lasted for many years. Scores of people were killed on both sides. It is said that in a single fight subsequently, on hundred people from both sides were killed.[39]

One of the triggering causes of the 30 years Rind-Lashaar war is said to be Gohar's camels. She was a *Baahot* of Mir Chaakar, the Rind Chief. The Lashaar killed her baby-camels after a row precipitated apparently after an unjust decision of Rind judges of a horse-race between Raamen Lashaar and Rehaan Rind. Mir Chaakar made war upon the Lashaar. He rejected the good counsel of Meeraan and Beebagr. He was adamant to teach a lesson to Lashaar tribe. He maintained that they had insulted the entire tribe by killing the camels of Gohar who was under his protection. The battle was lost by Mir Chaakar, but he did not accept the calumny that might have resulted if he did not act promptly on that provocation act of Lashaar.

Doda Gorgej fought against the better armed and superior number of men organized by Beebagr who had taken away the cows of Sammi, a *Baahot* of Doda. In the fight, Doda and all his men were killed. Baalaach, later on, avenged his brother's death. This affair remained an active feud for nearly 3 decades, and more than eighthly people lost their lives. According to traditions, a wealthy widow, Sammi settled in the village of Doda Gorgej and requested the privilege of *Baahot*. Beebagr, the puzh Sardar, wanted to recover from her some cows of Sammi's deceased husband who was his relative. He ordered his men to carry away some of her cows. Doda who was married a few days back and was at home, when informed of the happening, pursued the invading party and was killed. Mir Kambar gave his life in the battle because he did not allow Mir Mehraab to take people as prisoners and plunder their property who were living in Mir Kambar's area and impliedly were his *Baahot*.

Baahot could never to be refused, whatever may be the risk. Beebagr, a relative of Mir Chaakar was accorded protection by Mir Gwahraam, the hostile Lashaar Chief when he came with Graannaaz, the daughter of a Kandahar noble.[40] Mir Gwahraam gave refuge to one of his arch-

---

39 Muhammad Sardar Khan Baloch, A literary History of Balochis, pp. 474-475.

40 According to Baloch traditions, Beebagr went to Kandahar, most probably sent by Mir Chaakar on some diplomatic mission to Arghun court, with whom Mir Chaakar was on friendly terms. Zunnun Beg Arghun was the Viceroy of Sultan Husain Baikara of Herat (1468-1507 A.D). While in Kandahar, Beebagr developed a love affair with the daughter of the ruler of

enemy, very much aware of its disastrous consequences. The ruler followed Beebagr and came to Balochistan at the head of a strong army to rescue his daughter. The dispute was, however, resolved due to the exceptional bravery and courage of Beebagr himself who went to the tent of the encamped Sardar at night by killing the guards and submitted himself before him and asked his mercy for the grave insult and misdeeds he had committed. The ruler forgave him and gave the hand of Graannaaz to Beebagr. Giving protection to Beebagr by Mir Gwahraam and his determination to fight the superior enemy forces to defend his *Baahot*, the close relative of his arch-enemy, is one of the shining examples of the Baloch adherence to their traditional codes of honor.

Another example was the giving of refuge by the Khan of Kalat, Mir Mehraab Khan to the fleeing Afghan King, Shah Shujaul Mulk, after his defeat by Amir Dost Muhammad's forces at Kandahar on 2nd June 1834. The Shah fled to lash on the shore of the lake of Sistan. Later on, he made his way across the desert to Kalat.[41] He

---

Kandahar, and abducted his daughter Graannaaz, and brought her to Sibi. He took refuge with Mir Gwahraam, the Lashaar chief, who welcomed him as Baahot. The Kandahar ruler followed Beebagr with a strong army and came to Lashaar area. Rind and Lashaar armies assembled to fight the common enemy. Beebagr mindful of the outcome of such a disastrous battle, one night entered the tent of the encamped Afghan chief after killing the guards, and submitted himself personally to his mercy, deeply regretting the wrong he had done to him and requested his magnanimity. The king was very much impressed by the courage of Beebagr; and after consultations with his nobles, forgave him and even consented to the marriage of her abducted daughter with Beebagr. The ruler referred to, most probably, was Shah Beg son of Zunnun Beg. The event must have taken place before the Battle of Nali between Rind and Lashaar when the former were completely routed and consequently sought help of Arghun to take revenge upon the latter.

The entire episode as mentioned in Balochi ballads appears to be mythical and exaggerated. No such event has been reported either by Indian or Persian historians. There is no trace of any invasion of Sibi by the Arghuns only because of such an incident. An event of such a nature, involving the daughter of a ruler, could not go unnoticed by the historians of those time. The lady who was brought by Beebagr many have been a daughter of one of the Kandahar nobles or Sardar who might have pursued Beebagr with some followers and settled the issue amicably with the Baloch.

41   G.P. Tate, The Kingdom of Afghanistan: A historical Sketch, (First published in 1911 by Times press, Bombay) Pakistani edition: Indus Publications, Karachi,1973. p 135.

arrived at Kalat where Mir Mehraab Khan was encamped in a farm at Garadi, seven miles from Kalat. The Shah walked directly into his tent and asked his protection, as a Baahot, which was instantly granted. Meanwhile, the Afghan forces who were pursuing the Shah demanded that he should be handed over to them. Mir Mehraab Khan rejected the counsel of his political advisor, Daud Muhammad, who requested the Khan to deliver up the defeated prince to the Afghan General. Khan Mehraab khan sent a strongly worded message to the commander of the Afghan army, Rahm Dil Khan, to the effect that Shah Shuja had asked protection which had been promised according to Baloch traditions and that he would be protected by all means. He asked the Afghan General to immediately withdraw his troops from Kalat territory. As politically, Kalat was supposed to be under the Afghan King, Mir Mehraab Khan's action was a glaring example of the Baloch tradition.

Malik Khatee, the Chagai tribal chief gave refuge to Emperor Humayun. Not only did he resist the temptation to arrest the Mughal Prince and hand him over to the ruler of Kandahar at a high price but escorted him to the borders of Persia. He told the Mughal prince that as he was in his area he had the privilege of being a *Baahot* and that it was an insult to him if something happened to Humayun.

The simplest way of asking to be a *Baahot* was to enter the house premises of a Baloch and then demand protection. The Baloch not only defended the *Baahot* but even took to arms in order to restore any property already lost, or compensate to an injustice already done. There is an instance of Shahbek, a Rind noble's grievances against the Barozai ruler of Sibi, Jawan Bakhth, which resulted in eighteen battles between Baloch and the Barozais. Shahbek came to Kalat and requested the privilege of a *Baahot* of Mir Ahmad Khan I (1666-1695 AD). His son had been killed on the orders from Jawan Bakhth on the complaint from a trader who had alleged that Shahbek's son had forcefully removed his earnings. Without any further inquiry, the Barozai ruler had ordered the execution of Shahbek's son. After getting the status of a *Baahot*, he requested the help of the Khan in order to settle his score with the Barozai chief. The Khan declared war on Barozais. Eighteen battles were lost by the Khan's forces. During the fifteenth battle, the Khan's sister Mai Beebu was killed. However, the last two battles were decisively won by the Baloch army. The dispute was then resolved, and Shahbek was compensated according to the customs. It may be pointed out that the rivalry between the Khan and Barozai was deep-rooted and was on the question of sovereignty over Kachchi, which was under Barozais at that time. The Khan claimed the area as a part of the Khanate. The Barozais rejected the claim. However, the immediate cause of the war was the Shahbek affair.

Bier

To avenge the blood was the foremost duty of everybody. A Baloch never forgot to avenge the blood of his kin. Sometimes, the death ceremonies such as *purs*, which is a formal expression of grief over the death by the community, was postponed until the time when the blood was avenged. Beebagr avenged the death of his father by killing Shey Kattee, Mir Chaakar's Spirituals teacher, not taking into account the possible reaction of the powerful Chief.

Sometimes an unusual number of people were killed to avenge only one or a few persons. Baalaach killed over eighty people to avenge the death of his brother, Doda, and promised to kill more. Haarin killed a hundred people to avenge his two brothers Hasan and Mahmad. He killed one hundred persons from the enemy clan, counting ten for Hasan's sword, ten for his steed, ten for his ammunition, and ten for Mahmad and fifty for his blood.[42]

Head for a head was in the case of people of equal status. But compensating the death of a hero, Chief or a man of higher caste this rule was not followed; and more people from the offender's side were killed.

Blood was avenged mostly by close male relatives. In case there were no close relatives, it was generally, but not too often, avenged by clansmen or any member of the tribe. If the killer was a hired one or from low-caste, the motivator or conspirator was killed regardless of his position, after fully establishing that he was the cause of the

---

42 Sad murd gutgeerun kutha,
    Dah pa rahukin mahlawa,
    Dah pa lahmen kannawa,
    Dah pa mourthin jaabawa,
    Dah pa kasaanin Mahmada,
    Panja pa aishien sara.

perpetrated wrong. When the murderer was from the low-caste, the blood was compensated by killing more persons from the culprit's family and relatives. Another tradition was that the Baloch usually forgave the blood shed by a person of low status because they considered it inappropriate to avenge on a person who was not of the deceased's equal status.

Blood feud once created could turn into a tribal conflict which would continue for decades, killing many people from either side. Blood feuds among the tribes were settled by the elders who would go to the house of the aggrieved party with the relations of the offenders and theoretically accept the guilt and offer an unqualified apology. They would ask for the mercy of the victims' family in accordance with the traditions. Usually, the blood was forgiven after some formalities and exchanges of elderly advice. Among some tribes, the negotiators or *meid* offered some nominal compensation as a token of deep sympathy and regrets from the family or the clan who perpetrated the wrong which was generally accepted. There was no other way of settling blood disputes. Similar course to settle a row between two tribes was followed. If unsettled, the feud would continue from one generation to another. Regular debtor and creditor account were kept by both sides. Blood was never let unpaid. If there were no male relative to avenge the blood, the female members sometimes took up arms to avenge their dead member.

In Baloch code, it was an insult to accept any payment for the dead relative. He would simply pardon the offender and agree to symbolic compensation as an indication of grief and sympathy for the aggrieved family. It was almost impossible for him to bargain with the enemy. Baalaach waited for nearly eighteen years and then started his forays on the enemy. Mir Bijjaar avenged the defeat and death of his father, Mir Oumar, after a long time. Mir Oumar, the Mirwaadi chief was the Ruler of Surab and adjoining districts. Jam Shakar, a Jadgaal chief, collected a Lashkar from Kachchi to fight Mir Oumar, who was killed in a surprise attack on his capital, Nigadkot in circa 1515 A.D. Surab came under Jadgaal Chief. The widow of Mir Oumar, Bibi Maahaan along with her infant son, Mir Bijjaar fled away to Mastung where she had relatives. After many years when Bijjaar came of age, he expressed his desire to avenge his father's death. After receiving encouragements from his mother, he went to Surab in disguise, and with the help of Mirwaadi notables, defeated the Jadgaal nobles and captured Nigadkot.

A famous Balochi war ballad is a clear manifestation of not forgetting the murder of a relative:

> "Negotiations and arbitration could be possible when the palm of the hand grows hair: Jackal becomes the guard of the chickens or birds: lions are grazed with the camels; cotton could be noninflammatory; elephants are reduced to millet in size, and when fish could be found living outside waters. A Baloch would forego to avenge when tamarisk grows spikes (thorns) and snakes develop feet; lions are domesticated and boats are run through sands instead of waters; Sardars start the work of slaves and shepherds graze wolves[43].

An enmity once started never subsided. Blood must have to be paid in blood.

> "If stone could melt away in waters then the spirit of revenge could be subsided, but neither the stone melt away nor the spirit of revenge could be extinguished in Baloch heart. For two centuries it persists and remains smart like a young deer of tender age".[44]

---

43 Hama wahdaan mani (o) thai suhl (o) thraan bieth,
    (Ke) shagaal murg o kapothaani shipaank beith,
    Shikaraani pulang goun ushtheraan bieth,
    Agan pukki goun aasa ham kana bieth,
    Agan pill arzune daana kasaan bieth,
    Agan maahi redin danna thachaan bieth.
    Hama wahdaan mani (o) thai suhl (o) thraan bieth,
    Ke gazzaan kuntag o maraan paad,
    Boji man hama raikaan roth.
    Lao banth hama jangi sheir,
    Sardar diyanth langaaraan,
    Gurkaana shipaank chaarenanth,

44 sing agan chaathaani buna rezanth.
    Kenag cha mardaani dila kinzanth,
    Na sing rezanth na kenag Kinzanth,
    Bier Balochaani than do sad saala,
    Lassaen aahuge do danthaanin,

The Baloch approach to an enemy is fully depicted in a poem attributed to Baalaach who fought an entire tribe.

> *"I will do away with the evildoers, Doda's enemies, in a manner a falcon does to the pigeons; the way hot winds dry up small ponds; the way swine devastates millet crops; the way goats swallow up the branches of prosodies spacebar; the way wolf treats lambs and fisherman with river fishes".*[45]

Revenge had become a strong element in Baloch culture. It would become the prime aim of a lifetime or more. His entire life was reshaped and circled around one goal- to avenge the blood of his kin.

> *"Those who take revenge pass the sleepless night and stand alerted during the day; never act on the advice of a foe; forego all wealth and became ready to sacrifice his life.*[46] *How could he forget the murder of a great father or brother or any other*

---

45 Man goun badaan hanchu kanaan,
    Dodae joren duzhmenaan,
    Meid kananth goun maahiyaan
    Baanz goun kapothi wallaraan,
    Garmen lewaar goun chuluraan,
    Hukkin ladi goun arzunaan,
    Buz goun kaheeri dangaraan
    Gurk goun mazan chedin jadaan.

46 Aa mard ke bieraan geranth,
    Shap allahi bewaab banth,
    Roche dobar daah kananth,
    Pa duzhmenaan nishaan drushanth.
    Aa mard ke honaan Geranth
    Saanga nazuranth duzhmenaan,
    Panthaan chama joren badaan.
    Aa mard ke honaan geranth,
    Bezaar cha malaan banth,
    Aishi saraana zeyaan kananth.
    Aa mard ke hon o bier kananth
    Maahen janaan angaar kananth,
    Bachchaan goun shaagin gwanzagaan,
    Methaap o shaahi killagaan,
    Wabish talaraani sarenth,

relative when nobody would give up easily even a pie lost in the jungle?[47]

When a Baloch decides to take revenge, he directs all his energies to achieve that goal. He fixes a role for himself and for each of his family members. He foregoes any comfort and starts a relentless struggle. There is no comfort, no solace, and no peace. He visualizes the difficulties of hot weather and inhospitable places; far from the village, he hides away and wanders about. "His gonchan (kit-bag) and Kalli, waterskin, at times, become very burdensome to carry along. He drinks from hot ponds which even the wild deer hesitate to take".[48]

> "*Those who avenges blood make mountains their forts; high peaks their abode; lofty heights their place of comfort and inaccessible gorges their colleagues. They drink from the flowing springs using the leaves of Mediterranian dwarf palm as drinking cups; the spiky grass their place to rest upon, and hard ground their bed; their sandals serve as horses; trackless ravines their depositories. Their sons are arrows; sons-in-law are pointed daggers; their brothers are shields and fathers are double-edged swords*"[49].

---

47 Kas gabbare pa gaaria nelieth,
    Man wathi aaripin pithe biera,
    Choun killaan goun duzhmenin mardaan.

48 Chaake mani bier goun duzhminaan gaarenth,
    Kambarin gonchaan mani sara baarenth,
    Toba cha gonchaana dobandena,
    Kalliani bandaan warokenaan.
    Cha zihaani joshinthagin aapaan,
    (ke) saydish pa naakaami geranth thingaan.

49 Kohanth Balochaani kalaath,
    Burzen asiesh gwaathgeranth,
    Hamraahish beraahen garanth,
    Aapish bahoken chammaganth,
    Aapwaarish pishshi kundalanth,
    Neshthajaahish garkaawaganth,
    Bopesh dagaari thahthaganth,
    Boresh sawaasi chabbawanth,
    Bachchish gecheeni gondalanth,
    Zamathish shillein khanjaranth,
    Brathish thalaarein esparanth,

As long as his relative's blood remains unpaid and his *bier* or revenge is outstanding, he thinks himself as a man waiting for an opportune moment to take revenge. The mode of avenging the blood may differ and must be in the same proportion in which the first murder took place. If inhuman or insulting tactics were adopted in the killing, the revenge would be of the same nature. There was no leniency in this regard. If somebody was beaten to death he was avenged in the same manner. Bijjaar, a sixteenth-century nobleman was killed by Buledais. His ribs were roasted to feed the birds. Bijjaar's relatives killed the Buledai Chief, Haibithaan; his head was cut off, his skull was fashioned into drinking cup.[50]

Even after the settlement of a murder dispute, it was painful for the relatives of the deceased to carry on normal relations with the enemy. Sometimes, to settle the dispute permanently, the offender's relatives gave a lady in marriage to the aggrieved family. This was to be in the case where the offender held a superior or equal position in the social hierarchy. This was, however, resorted to minimize the chances of any future eruption of the enmity between the parties on some other pretexts. It may, however, be pointed out that once the case of blood feud was settled it would not be considered desirable to take revenge. The revenge then would be a grave deviation from normal practice. Therefore, such a feud could break out in some other shape because of persistent hatred between the parties.[51]

In avenging blood, any method could be adopted which was considered necessary. Baalaach used hit-and-run tactics in his struggle against an entire tribe. Mir Chaakar brought in aid from Arghuns who devastated the whole region. Bijjaar avenged his father, Oumar's death through a stratagem. However, it was a normal principle that before attacking, the victim was warned and reminded of his guilt because deceitful manners were generally considered below Baloch status. In a tribal dispute, he always fought face to face with proper warnings to each side.

Aarip mazan tappein ludanth.

50 Muhammad Sardar Khan Baloch, A literary history of the Balochis, Vol I, P. 320

51 Honi dobar dosth nabieth,
    Peth kushthenaan hosth nabieth.

Shigaan

Baloch always behaved in a respectable and honorable manner. His entire behavior was guided by a strict social code. Any weakness or action which was not in accordance with social ethos was scornfully rebutted by the people. Such a rebuttal was considered a great insult. *Shigaan* or taunting was an established factor in Baloch culture and a permanent check on its members. It was a frank and honest opinion of others about others. Everybody was conscious lest he was jibed at for any undesirable action not only of his own but of his family and friends. If inadvertently he committed a mistake or any step taken by his family members, it was promptly judged and decided upon and immediately ridiculed scornfully. Such scoff would usually be directed against the person at *Diwaan* or on ceremonial occasions. A person whose wife was suspected to be unfaithful would receive directly or indirectly the derisive contempt of others. If somebody failed to avenge the blood of his relative, he was always looked down upon with hatred and mocked at. If anybody ran away from the battlefield, he was cursed and his action was remembered even after his death, and his sons received the appropriate taunting. The Baloch was never afraid of death but greatly abhorred to live a life of disgrace. One dies once, but if the living is taunted a hundred times it is no doubt far worse than death. *'Marg yek roch o shigaan sad roch'*, therefore *shigaan* was unbearable.

Mir Gwahraam, the Lashaar chief, jeered at Mir Chaakar, the chief of Rind tribe for his defeat, boasting that since he had killed Meeraan along with a score of Rind fighters, Chaakar was now fit for a shepherd's role. Gwahraam said Rind was routed because Chaakar lacked the acumen and capacity to make wise decisions. This was an insult for Chaakar who promised to avenge his defeat.

Bibi Baanadi's taunting to Baloch Lashkar in the battle of Panipat not only brought the entire Baloch forces in fierce fighting but ultimately influenced the fate of the battle. The mother of Doda taunted him saying that those who kept *Baahot* would never sleep at ease and let the *Baahot* be molested or her property taken away. Doda immediately got up, followed the raiding party and in the process was killed. Graannaaz sent a message to her husband Lalla, promising him not to be his wife anymore because she was hurt and ashamed by the news that he had run away from the battlefield. She expected her husband to fight like a lion and fall in the battle like other brave men. It was against her sense of honor to remain the wife of a coward because she had boasted a few days earlier about the bravery of her husband which proved wrong. The story goes like this:

Graannaaz, daughter of Mir Baaraan, a nobleman of Kalmath, was married to Lalla. A few days after their marriage, Baaraan and his sons had to fight an old enemy. Lalla also decided to fight on the side of his father-in-law. During the fight, Baaraan and his sons were killed while Lalla received grievous injuries and was about to fall from the horse back when his trusted servant whipped his horse away to save his life. Reports came to Graannaaz that her father and brothers had been killed. The proud lady was told that while the battle was going on, Lalla had withdrawn from the fight and had fled away. This was the gravest insult to Graannaaz who could not think of her husband as a coward. She had boasted before her friends that Lalla would be among the first few brave people to be killed in the battle. She swore not to accept Lalla as her husband.[52]

It is said that when after several days of discussions on the course of action which was to be taken against the Lashaar who killed Gohar's camels and insulted the Rind, the majority of Rind nobles were in favor of declaring war against Lashaar. Only a few including Meeraan and Beebagr were against this disastrous expedition. Beebagr opposed war maintaining that they could not let their men be killed for that Jat's camels. Some braggarts passed sarcastic remarks towards Beebagr, saying that he was a coward. Mir Chaakar himself said Beebagr might be afraid of arrows and broad-bladed Indian swords of Lashaar fighters. He jibed at him saying that they would put him at a safe distance far from the battlefield.[53] This was a great insult for a

---

52 Pahr basthag(man) payrien rocha,
    Goun wathi jaani dazgwahaarukkaan,
    (Ke) kaith thai sheeri kusthene ahwaal,
    Goun sari warnahaan thalaanginaan,
    (Guda man) nill kanaan kulle har chahaar surugaan,
    Dar kanaan prah kundin kadoligaan,
    Gosh bunaani paaresthagin durraan,
    Drusthan yak graanen hukkahe shepaan,
    Sarmusebaththin medahe nendaan.

53 Beebagr goundalaan srahmenthag,
    Hindiyaan machande daathag,
    Uda ke janoun ma zahmaan,

brave man like Beebagr; he agreed to command and fought against the Lashaar.

Sado sent a taunting message to Kiyya, her beloved, calling him a liar because he did not turn up as promised by him. Kiyya getting the message immediately came to Sado traveling scores of miles in one night.

One of the six daughters of Mir Naseer Khan, Gulnaaz, who was hunch-backed, asked her father not to give her in marriage to anybody lest someone taunted him because of her deformity.

Lajj o Mayaar

The term connoted a penetrating philosophical abstraction and meant Baloch adherence to his high principles in all matters. In its general sense, it was a comprehensive term having deep cogitative, metaphysical, social and ethical standards. In other words, it was intelligent self-restraint on certain matters, and a vigorous and provocative force demanding the individual to act and behave in a manner prescribed by the tribal codes. It was the disciplinary inner-strength of the individual regulating his entire conduct. While *Lajj o Mayaar* connoted all the best qualities, *Belajj*, or person devoid of *lajj*, had all the characteristics of a vicious and a contemptible person of wicked nature. Figuratively, however, the very word, Baloch, or Balochi meant *Lajj o Mayaar*. It depicts the traditions of justice and equality, reasonableness and sobriety, bravery and courage, sagacity and wisdom, truthfulness and honesty, and hospitality and devotion.

Mehr

A Baloch hated the enemy to the extreme but had the highest regards and affection for those he liked. *Mehr*, deep devotion and

---

Thirdouri thara durneyadun,
Theeraan huzai guwazinun,
Julle thai sara perrenun,
Maa o zahm janin Lashaari,
Aap o bannawi maan kaahum,
Hoshag penj kanoun ipthiay,
Nend o gend kai soub bieth.

extreme possessive love, was the guiding spirit and provided virtually a sound base for his outlook. His regard for his family and friends was profound. He was devoted to those who may have helped him in any manner, *'Thaase aap ware sad saala wapa bedaar'*: you should have affection for the person for a century who once offered you a glass of water, so goes an old Balochi maxim. He never raised hand on the person from whose house he had taken meals. Beebagr refused to eat food served by Mir Gwahraam during his stay as *Baahot* after the kidnapping episode of Graannaaz. His reason was that as enemies they would be fighting very soon. How could he then fight Gwahraam after eating in his house?

Veneration of war heroes

Bravery and courage were the only criteria for getting respect from the common folk. Everybody was full of praise for the men who fell in the battle. Minstrels composed verses in their honor and women sang those in their time of loneliness or as lullabies to their kids. Those who ran from the battlefield were always cursed and dubbed as not sons of their true fathers. Their relatives and friends considered their cowardliness as a great insult to them.

Baloch war songs are full of accounts of the war heroes who showed exemplary courage. Mir Kambar who gave battle to Mir Mehraab; Baalaach who revenged upon his brother's murderer; Lalla who fought to remove a misunderstanding of his wife Graannaaz and a host of others are the heroes in Baloch history who created names in war and peace. Mir Siyah Sawaar, Mir Jalalaan, Mir Chaakar, Mir Gwahraam, Mir Naseer Khan, Khan Mir Mehraab Khan, and Mir Baloch Khan Noshervani have been accorded great respect in Baloch traditions. Bibi Baanadi and Mai Beebu are the revered ladies for their courage on the battlefield. The former is believed to have commanded and fought on the side of Emperor Humayun in the battle of Panipat, and the latter was killed in the fight against the Baarozais of Sibi. There are scores of others who earned eternal fame in the Baloch annals.

The Baloch loved to be killed in the battle and earn lasting glory and become a legend. The Baloch stubborn resistance and bold fight in the battle of Miyani against the superior British forces; the determined gallantry of seven hundred Bugtis who fought Merewether's horsemen and let themselves be killed than surrender, fully reflect the Baloch attitude towards heroism. We find that Baloch fighting the Iranian might during the Sassanid period perished but refused to submit. Leaders of some Baloch tribes picked up a rivalry with the Kerman ruler in late 9th century A.D; they preferred migration *en masse* than accept the insulting terms for a settlement with him.

The Baloch son was nursed and taught to be a war hero. It was the only desire of his mother and sister. The mother confidently thought of those days in her lullaby when her son would come to the age, ride on horseback, having sword, shield, and fight the enemy when need be. This was also the wish of his proud sister who boasted of having a brother because those who had no brothers were unfortunate and deserved death:

> *Aa Gwahaara ke thangahen braath niest goun kulla syah suchaath.*

A brother may be a very mean person yet for a sister he was to be revered because affection for him exceeds everything:

> *Braath agan legaar o pachaar maathe, mehre cha kullen aalama zeyathin.*

And after all, sons or brothers are gifted from the Heaven and only the luckiest could have them (*If they were goods to be purchased none except the wealthy princes could obtain them. The poor's share would have been only grief and deep frustration*).[54] If a woman bore a son, everybody in the family was happy and celebrated it. The mother was proud of herself because she had borne a son-a valuable gift from the Heavens, a light which had beautified everything; her house and its premises and the pendulum.[55]

---

54 Bachch o bahth bahaai bothien,
   Maaldaar o mugemaan zurthien,
   Bemaal goun gamaan gimurthien.

55 Bachchi buthag o man disthag,
   Chammana do rouk maan buthag,
   Mulke mardumaan gal zurthag,
   Kaapar chou gerouke rouka,
   Peishgaah chu suhaile shahma,
   Kull goun guwaanzaga shahm gepthag.

The village ladies who gathered in the house of the mother congratulated her and sang *sepath* (songs of praise) for the mother and the child because she was lucky to give birth to a son who would create a name in glory.[56] He was expected to be hospitable and protector of the helpless. He was constantly taught by the mother to follow the path of bravery and earn a name for himself and his forefathers. His mother sings him lullabies wishing him to be a man of exceptional courage, always firm in the saddle. She wished him to die only in the battlefield because it never behoved brave men to die in the bed.

> *Dear- heart, True- heart,*
> *God makes thee brave-heart.*
> *Thine be a steed of fiery mettle,*
> *Thine be a seat firm in the saddle,*
> *Four fair wives mayst thou embrace;*
> *Milk- white, Honey-sweet, sun-bright, Moon- face.*
> *Thine be no death on the bed of a craven,*
> *For death on the field is the road to Heaven.*
> *Dear- heart, True- heart,*
> *God makes thee brave-heat.*[57]

From the very childhood, a son would boast among his friends that he would behave in the manner his mother expected him in her lullabies: live like a warrior and die in the battle-field with honors.

The Baloch used a unique way to show their resolution to fight to the end. On many occasions, they bound themselves into a group so that nobody could detach himself and give in. When Mari tribesmen fought the British troops at Hadab in 1918, twenty miles from Mawand, a group of them bound themselves with an injured Mari elder, Mir Khudadaad, to show their determination to fight to the last. Another practice was to vow that if he returned without victory or without the goals aimed at the fight his wife was considered divorced. Yet another way was to divorce one's wife before the battle

---

56 Laaka man thai Baahotaan,
    Kapthoka mani jaandrah kan,
    Washanth dour hama bachchaani,
    Doldarien saki mulkaani,
    Sawaar beith markabaan juannenaan
    (Goun) raaji wajahaan kanenaan,

57 Denys Bray, The life History of a Brahui, p. 22.

in an exceptional determination to be either killed or return victorious. Mir Kambar divorced his wife he had married a few days earlier before going to the battle with the remark that if he was killed she was free to choose a match: and if he survived he would take her back. In the Rind-Lashaar battle of Nali, Rind did not run away from the battle because they were bound by the promise they had with their glorious wives.[58] When Beebagr was arguing with the Chief regarding the futility of the battle with the Lashaar who were gathering in large numbers to fight the Rind, some youths while jeering for his cowardly reservations on the outcome of the war, bound themselves with high oaths to fight against Lashaar.

A mother sang for her son visualizing the day when he would have a beautiful mare and fight the enemy because the death on the battlefield was the road to eternal fame. Mir Kambar's mother expected him to create a name in bravery so that his grandfather's soul could rest in peace and his father become proud of himself.[59] She told her son that if he died in the battlefield, she would lament his death with all happiness and bear again a son of his caliber.[60] Doda's mother told him that he should rather be killed than let Sammi's cows be carried away by the enemy. Bibi Maahaan, the mother of Mir Bijjaar Mirwaadi, was overjoyed when she heard her son planning to avenge his father's death from the Jadgaals though she was fully aware of the danger to the life of her only son. According to traditions, she told her son that she had nursed him so well only to see this courage and determination from him. She joyfully presented him with the sword of his father and asked him to keep it as a sacred trust and as a symbol of his ancestral bravery.

---

58 Rind nathathkanth ke Rind mayaar daaranth,
   Dashthagaan luddoken jani ahdaan.

59 Bachchi mani chamme chiraag,
   May didag o zirday muraad,
   Zahm jan o nama daraar,
   Nam thai pithe washnaam bieth,
   Kabr piruke amboh bieth.

60 Bachchi agan janga mere,
   (Guda) Nokin saro gwaape kanaan,
   Kahaan thai kabre saraa,
   Mothke badal haalo kanaan.
   Thai matta dobar peda kanaan

The Baloch mother was deeply proud of her son who when came to age smartly dressed, would have the usual six armaments: sword, shield, spear, dagger, bow and a quiverful of arrows, always ready to fight. He would enjoy a place of respect among the people. In her imagination, she accorded him an important place where the chief would call for her brave son in a time of emergency. He would explain to him the grave crisis and the nature of fight with the enemy who would gather in great strength. Then she advises her son:

> "Show exceptional courage, make use of your sword and bow, and prove yourself a true Baloch. This is what is expected of you. As a sister has confidence in a brother or hopes for a reunion with her remote family, and a girl has trust in her lover, the nation has faith in you and awaits the report of your deeds. Have regard to this advice of your mother".[61]

---

61 Leel o leel kanith bachaara,
  Bachch mani pul gudin warna bieth,
  Bandith har shashien athyaraan,
  Zahm o thupak o Kaataraan,
  Neza esparanth pa kaaraan,
  Zurith jabawaan morthinaan,
  Thaachith markabaan thrundinaan,
  Jorin duzhminaan parramith,
  Badwahaan shakundem kanth,
  Nendith medwaan komiyaan.
  Sardar kasside shaksaith,
  Beyahith o gihin warnahaan,
  Jangginth (goun) duzhminaan jorenaan,
  Dehe zaalemin badwahaan,
  Zurith ugdowaan graninaan,
  Jumbeneth hazaari pojaan,
  Bandig kaneth honiyaan.
  Ae ni gwashthananth maathie,
  Jang e saahathaan granenaan,
  Zahma goun watha sasaakan,
  heelanth pathai shaaroan,
  Gwahaar pa derawaan durenaan,
  Kaad pa sammalaan koliyaan,
  Koum pa thai Balochi naama,
  Math pa daathagen lollian,
  Leel o leel mani bachchaara,
  Bachch o sad muraadin laala.

111

The mother or sister in their *Zaheerok*, melancholy songs, sung in times of loneliness for relatives who are abroad or on long journeys; described the son or brother as a great noble. Now think of the mother or sister expecting the arrival of her son or brother after a long time. In her imagination, she describes the arrival of a ship which is carrying her son. The following Zaheerok has pageant impressions with deep effects. The cannotativeness of the words take the reader from the world of imagination to near actuality. One can feel the extreme affection and deep pride she has for that man:

> *O look, there approaching a ship,*
> *Traveling in it is a glorious son of a (proud) mother;*
> *A brother revered by a sister,*
> *A husband loved by many princesses (wives)*
> *Look, now coming out meds and jaanshus,*
> *Disembarking great youth of a people;*
> *Slowly and gracefully reaching the bay,*
> *I recognize my son amongst many smartly dressed nobles.*[62]

During marriage ceremonies he was highly praised for his courage, hospitality, and humility:
Halo haalo for the dressed prince,
Halo haalo for the brave,
Halo haalo for the generous and hospitable,
Halo haalo for his sword and dagger,
Halo haalo for his *lajj o mayaar,*
Halo haalo for the princely Baloch,
Halo haalo for our great hope[63]

---

62 Dour bichaareth ke maile pedaakenth,
    Mannenthe maathi thangahen bachche,
    Yak gwahaari dousth daashtaaagen braathe,
    Shah janaani yak dilsaren joude.
    Dar rechanth med o dar rechanth jaanshu,
    Dar kapant raaji bringinen warna,
    Man wathi bachcha man pulgudin miraan drusth kanaan.

63 Halo haalo kanith mira yalena,
    Halo haalo kanith mir pul gudina,
    Halo haalo kanith sherin mazaara,
    Halo haalo kanith darya dilaara,
    Halo haalo kanith zahm o kataara,

War ethics

Among the Baloch, the war was always glorified through national traditions. *Soub goun shakkalien jangaananth*: "victory is with sweet wars" is a true manifestation of Baloch attitude towards war. It is deeply rooted in their culture and language. War against the enemy either for defense or to avenge a wrong was always treated as honorable and righteous. Heroism and courage were glorified, while passiveness and cowardice were condemned as effeminate and defamatory: *'heyraani thuman veeraananth'*, the tribes who are docile face the doom.

The Baloch approach to war was not purposeless violence but mainly the reaction to injustice, individual or collective. It was conditioned usually by external factors. A Baloch was peaceful as long as he did not see any danger to his security or honor. Once he was convinced that a threat existed, he would start a constant struggle which may take any shape: an open fight or hit-and-run methods.

The wars in ancient times were complete for the losers: men put to death, the women kept slaves, boys castrated, cattle taken way, and buildings damaged or razed to the ground. But the Baloch war was total for the combatants only. Battles were usually fought outside the settlements. In their intertribal wars, they never took the Baloch women as slaves nor did they enter into the houses after a victory on the battlefield.

The Baloch always fought face to face. Deceitful or devious tactics were hardly adopted, apart from usual legitimate tactics to divert the attention of the enemy from one side and attack from the other.

The horse had been one of the main instruments of war. The battle dress appears to be a normal tribal dress. The large *paag* (turban) has its usefulness in the war in protecting the head from the sword-cuts. At some stages in history, the Baloch might have used *zirra* (the coat of mail or chain mail) for body protection. As an excellent marksman, he used the arrow very effectively; however, the sword was the main weapon of war. The war techniques must have been influenced by indigenous methods. Persian and Indian influence was also clearly visible, especially in armament and war maneuvers. In

---

Halo haalo kanith lajj o mayaara,
Halo haalo kanith shaahen Balocha,
Halo haalo kanith may maah o rocha.

Balochi classical poetry, there are numerous references to swords from Khurasan or India, and shields from Sistan.

The Baloch never believed in the primitive combat tactics of many peoples, that is, an invasion of a hostile settlement at dawn, at night or with the aim of destroying it, killing the inhabitants including women and children. He always preferred open combat. The Baloch recognized certain persons, women, children and old people as non-combatants and never killed them. However, his tactics in warfare also included the element of surprise. He used his own war codes and indications.

One of the striking points in war ethics was that great respect was accorded to the leader of the opposing forces. Mir Chaakar in the battle of Nali was rescued by a Lashaar, Nodbandag. Various versions, however, of the background of the rescue[64] have been indicated in the folk traditions, but saving the Sardar from the enemy forces who were at that time still fighting could only be seen through the Baloch sense of respect to the leader who was fighting them. According to another tradition, when Mir Chaakar with the help of Kandahar rulers crushed the Lashaar, he erected a small tower out of the heads of the fallen foes, as he had pledged to do that. When a minstrel pointed to a gap in the head arrangements and addressed Mir Chaakar, saying that the head of Mir Gwahraam (the chief of Lashaar) deserved to be placed there, Chaakar got enraged and instantly killed the man and put his head on the place which was indicated by the minstrel, saying how could he conceive the head of glorious Gwahraam to be cut and placed there. He could not contemplate such an insult even to his bitter enemy.

War leaders who showed magnanimity to the defeated leaders are praised in folk literature. Sometimes the major theme in a story

---

64 Nodbandag when asked to explain his conduct by the Lashaar, had said that the entire victory would have been tasteless without Mir Chaakar living and mourning for the death of Meeraan and others. However, it is widely believed that Mir Gwahraam had ultimately approved Nodbandag's action. Because he did not take any action against a possible traitor, fully indicates the highest respects he gave to Chaakar. According to another version, Nodbandag refuted the allegation to be a Rind in disguise and thus a foe. He had maintainded that his mother Mudi, was a Rind who might have sung a lullaby at cradle saying you may be helpful to Mir Chaakar. One day Chaakar might need you when he would be in distress in a battle. He thus fulfilled the wishfull thinking of his mother.

is how a defeated Sardar or leader was treated with respect. Those who do not accord due respect to the opponents were selected for the role of either villain or painted as low castes. In war ballads, generals and heroes of the opposing army are always praised. Rind-Lashaar conflict continued for nearly three decades with many hot contests. But the ballads composed on either side[65] are full of the words and phrases which show that the Baloch generally never used slanderous or derogatory words even against his enemy. Mir Gwahraam always used appropriate words not only for Mir Chaakar but also for other war heroes like Meeraan. For Meeraan, he uses phrases such as invincible and glorious. He addresses Mir Chaakar as the 'Mighty Chief' and says of him like an evergreen tree, even after his disastrous defeat. For Gwahraam words used are noble, great and smartly dressed; and for Lashaar generally as a brave people. Beebagr calls the Lashaar *zahm janin Lashaar*, which means great fighters.

There are numerous examples where the enemy was never ridiculed. Baabar-e-Suhrab Dodai when addressed Mir Bijjaar whose hostility with Dodais continued for over a decade with many battles, calls him a brave man. A poem attributed to Haaro Mandost calls Bijjaar a courageous person adept in the use of the sword. In the same poem, Rinds are described as smartly dressed in white. While visualizing the position in a would be battle between Rind and Dodai, the poet praises the brave and invincible warriors of both sides. A ballad constructed by Haarin Bugti on the battle between Dreshak and Zarkaani Bugtis, he praises the courage and bravery of Dreshaks and their allies. Similarly, a poem on the battle between Mazaari and Gorchaani tribes where Mazaaris defeated their opponents, Gorchaani fighters have been equally lauded for their bravery in the battlefield. This is a unique characteristic of the Baloch which has amazing parallels only in some Hindu epics. In the Geeta, there is a description of the leaders and armies of Pandavas and Kurus, narrated by Sanjaya to King Dhritarashtra. The leaders and generals of the Kurus army

---

65 In a poem attributed to Mir Chaakar in connetion with Rind-Lashaar conflict there appear some derogatory words used for Gwahraam and the Lashaar in general. These must be later addition by bards to flatter the victorious Rind. It may be noted that neither Chaakar nor Gwahraam were poets. There are many poems ascribed to many Baloch heroes. Such poems were undoubtedly composed by bards, generally after many years of the events descrided.

are referred by name as great soldiers and famous men of war. They are praised for their determination to fight on the side of the Kurus. Similarly, the leaders and men of the opposing Pandavas are highly lauded as heroes and great bowmen. The chief of the enemy forces, the son of King Drupada, is referred to as the wise disciple of Guru Drona, and the king himself as a valiant King.[66]

Major points in Baloch war ethics included the following:

- The sanctity of home was never violated.
- Low castes, minstrels, and clergymen were never killed.
- Noncombatant old people, minors, women.
- An injured foe was never put to death.
- Persons who ran away from the battlefield were never pursued and killed.

The Baloch had some peculiar cultural traits and social ethos. There was immense importance on the individual who was highly egoistic and deeply proud. The respects for the brave while despising the coward was an important social behavior. Expressing respect for a fallen hero, even belonging to the enemy is something unique. A Baloch hates the enemy from the core of his heart but has the greatest regard for those whom he feels considerate towards him. Truthfulness, honesty, keeping one's vows and avenging an injustice were the cherished cultural values among them. The Baloch war ethics with much human face differentiated them from their medieval neighbors.

---

66 The Geeta, Trans: Purohit Swami, Faber and Faber Limited, London.1973, pp.15-16.

FOUR

RELIGION AND MYTHOLOGY

Religion is a commitment to a kind or quality of life recognizing a supernatural source and involving a wide range of human behavior. It has its domain in a series of human conduct: in culture, traditions, morality, law, and philosophy. Historically, it is a system of experiences, ideas, teachings and ritual practices, the nucleus of which is a belief in a supernatural being. Religion combines certain intrinsic feelings and emotions such as wonder, fear, and reverence. It tends to show a deep concern for self imposed values and morals. The custodians of religion always seek appropriate action embodying those values which they consider necessary. They characterize a human being and his conduct as good or bad, holy or unholy, virtuous or unvirtuous, godly or ungodly.

The God or supernatural being is believed to award appropriately for good conduct and punish invariably through calamities, sickness, death, and sufferings to those who deviate from the prescribed course of spiritual and moral conduct. This view has been conveniently enlarged to include entire groups of people who are said to succeed in worldly undertakings and achieve prosperity if they follow the teachings of God through His messengers. Misfortune on a people categorized as god-fearing has always been attributed very ludicrously to the wrongdoings of some earlier generations of those people.[1]

Worship and sacrifice are generally thought to be the basic universal elements in religious life. Worship is an overt reaction to man's experiences of the supernatural power and proper response to his

---

1   Num,14: 18 and Lev,26:39-42.

inner self. It is a service to the transcendent reality aimed at enriching and renewing closer relations with Him, upon which man feels hopeless and dependent. Sacrifice is regarded as a symbolic act which also establishes a firm liaison between men and the Sacred order. All important human occasions such as birth, puberty, marriage, death have been regarded as proper times for sacrifices with symbolic ramifications of man's status. Worship and sacrifice have been the main phenomenon in the religious history of mankind, which centre around the basic idea of human salvation which, in its earliest form, maybe the close spiritual relationship with ultimate Reality and ensuring safety for the human being and his deliverance or redemption from negative or disabling conditions such as death or misery. These conditions had been viewed to be the result of the wrath of the supernatural power.

Religions if analyzed in their proper historical perspective was neither good nor bad. They may be good as well as bad, depending on a lot of other objective conditions. Some religious belief might have been appreciable and useful for an individual or groups some thousand years ago but appear obnoxious today and vice versa. With the changes in human thought coupled with socio-economic and political development, the entire realm of religious outlook has undergone a transformation; and the process is still continuing, Mystery cults associated mainly with religion also appear to be crumbling in the wake of scientific and technological progress.

In ancient times, climatic conditions and certain other features of the region had often led to more subtle adaptations of cultural life, and in fact, have been the principal factors in shaping religious belief of primitive peoples. That is why certain religions in certain areas may have many points in common, while there are great deals of differences in the religions of the people who live in geographically different locations.

Religion is undoubtedly the response to man's intrinsic curiosity about the unknown. Religious practices such as worship or other rituals are usually prompted by man's fear complex and sense of insecurity. Human worship of Sun, Moon, Fire or wild animals fully indicates this phenomenon.

Certain religious practices, nevertheless, are the outcome of socio-economic factors. For example, fasting might have had its rationale from the paucity of food supply during certain seasons in the ancient past. In remote ages, special days or periods appear to have been set aside for fasting when there was a shortage of food, and for feasting when the supply increased. This practice was necessitated by economic conditions, though later on, it got religious sanction. Similarly, certain religious rituals celebrated seasonally were later on adopted by many as pre-requisites for an individual's spiritual or moral well being.

Myth is a basic constituent of religion[2] and may have spread by way of diffusion, or it may be the independent working of human imagination when confronted with very complex situations. Myths may not have been invented deliberately whose genesis is slow and most probably, unconscious. These might have grown into acceptance as unquestionable facts through many generations. It is a kind of communication, a religious symbolism which has specific accounts concerning gods or superhuman beings and objects connected with them. These are extraordinary events of circumstances altogether different from those of ordinary human experiences.[3] They illustrate religious doctrines and re-affirm a standard behavior. A myth explains not only the national, social, cultural and biological facts of a people; it could be regarded as a complete history. It depicts the peoples' outlook besides answering questions regarding the origin of rituals and practices. All the great religions of the world save Buddhism which did not oppose myth, are generally and sometimes ambiguously opposed to mythologics. The Muslim scripture, The Quran which derives its mythological contents mainly from the Old Testament, is critical of myths, though it has refined and explained many myths and tried to bring them closer to religious reality. The Jewish religion was critical of myths in many respects, and also Christianity. But these religions could not discard it from religious thought altogether.

Religion and mythology cannot be separated from primitive culture. They had a tremendous influence on a wide range of man's

---

2   The fundamental difficulty in religious understanding is to evolve a proper balance between intellegibility and mystery. This is perhaps the only base for deep controversy. If separated from rational thinking, religion will surely lose not only its true essence but also its vitality in an era of scientific and technological advancement.

3   Like religion, myths are the product of human glaring imagination to satisfy its deep curiosity about things or situations beyoud ordinary comprehension. Its domain is unknown. The cardinal point in the study of myth is to analyse the aim of the primitive mind by such myths and the goal intended to be achieved. Myths, no doubt, are extremely helpful in knowing the primitive peoples' outlook on a wide range of subjects.

social conduct. Many religious beliefs became the basis of most social practices. For example, belief in the supernatural power of the ruler caused him to be viewed as the protector of his tribe. The Chief, consequently, became the final authority in all matters pertaining to his people. Religion, however, very often acted as a retarding factor in human material development because, whenever confronted with novelty, it always became rigid and opposed social and cultural progress.

Religions had immense utility for primitive people, and have still not lost their importance for the modern mind because they are fulfilling man's spiritual requirements. For instance, belief in the supernatural being or in the power of ancestral spirits acted as a force of social control in many primitive societies. Therefore, the basis of most religious convictions may be an illusion, but the belief itself may be highly valuable.

Religions in their earliest forms could be regarded as a quest in search of a common spiritual goal, and as fulfilling a pressing need of the primitive people. There was, at first, no conflict or intolerance among various cults as was witnessed in the form of holy wars with barbarous ferocity in the subsequent stages of religious history. The contemporary organized religions such as Judaism, Christianity, and Islam, have a record of intolerance and persecution, especially the later, in the primary stage of its development as a socio-political system. It persecuted the followers of so-called wrong religions and infidels.

The genesis of Baloch religious beliefs

The Baloch religious and mythological history unto the Christian era is shrouded in obscurity. Nothing scientifically sound can be deduced from the sketchy records available. However, the main sources which give much evidence on Baloch history or religious beliefs are their cultural traditions preserved mainly in folk-literature. Here also a particular problem is faced by every historian for any intelligent use of this vast literature, mostly still unwritten, for deduction and logical analysis keeping in view the overall geographical and historical realities.

After their migration from the Caspian Sea region, the Baloch vanished from the historical accounts and only came into limelight after many centuries. Obviously, great pressure must have been brought on their religious and mythological outlook throughout these years by the indigenous peoples with which they interacted. They were also influenced by the religious faiths of ruling powers or the generalized religious or mythological influences of the region, especially of the Middle East. Therefore, any objective inquiry into their religion and mythologies cannot be regarded proper and helpful in a deeper understanding of it without a brief account of the indigenous peoples of areas where the Baloch had settled and came into contact with them. Their religion must invariably have had a great impact on Baloch religious beliefs and cultural behavior. It may also be pointed out that we have almost the same problem of unavailability of authentic historical record save a few deductions from archaeological findings and certain historical guesswork regarding the people and their civilization inhabiting Balochistan [4] from the earliest times up to the Aryan invasion of the subcontinent and the adjoining regions beginning from 1500 B.C.

The earliest radiocarbon date for settlement in Balochistan has recently been established at 7000 B.C. At the time, the region had a highly developed culture comparable to the world's many primitive civilizations. The excavations reveal the trace of an extremely ancient society of herdsmen who found abundant bush forages and water in different valleys for their flocks of goats, sheep, and cattle. They lived in houses of mud bricks. Instead of pottery, they used skin bags and baskets. They carried on limited agriculture and had tools made of stone. It is believed that these semi-tribal nomads learned the art of pottery making during the fifth or sixth millennium B.C. Their pottery was, however, crude and coarsely painted; most of it was molded inside basketry frames. It appears that the technology of pottery-making was coincidental with considerable achievements

---

4   The modern writer no doubt face great inconveniences in reconciling the accounts of Greek or Arab historians regarding geographical conditions of Balochistan or the people and their culture. Many natural features of the region, such as river bastions, land fertility or routes must have witnesed tremendous changes. This is fairly evident from excavations which show that Balochistan had many fertile valleys which produced human settlements with prospering cultures. Climatic conditions in Mehr Gad and Surab which are hot and cold respectively at present, must have been pleasant in the remote past. Both the regions were seats of some ancient civilizations.

in the field of agriculture by the beginning of the fourth millennium B.C. The attraction of fertile soil and water supply of valleys served as an impetus and resulted in more extensive settlements. Further improvement in technology shifted the emphasis from herding to agriculture. The hand-made pottery was declining and being replaced by highly sophisticated wheel wares. It is certain that copper was worked out and used during this period.

The third millennium B.C was an era of extensive settlement and development throughout the region. The villages were larger in size and their number had increased. The houses were small but passages between them were fairly widened. Doors were swung on stone sockets. Flat stone and pebbles were employed as foundations for mud brick walls. Hearths were also made in room floors. Though cattle rearing were still important for the economy, agriculture was at its climax during the final phases of the pre-historic period. Small mother goddess figurines obtained from the ritual buildings also emphasize the role of agriculture. Wheat and barley were most probably the principal crops.

Ethnological studies show that the earliest population of the subcontinent and its adjoining areas comprised of nearly four major races at various stages of early history. The measurements carried out on mummified skulls from the Naal have established that they belonged to the Mediterranean type. It is generally believed that the earliest were Negrito, followed by proto-Australoid and Mongoloid. The Aryan was the last racial group who penetrated on a large scale in the middle of the second millennium B.C. It is conjectured that about the beginning of the second millennium B.C. an extensive drought might have caused the collapse of the economic structure and the entire civilization before the Aryan eruption.

Evidence is also available, mostly from excavations; of important cultural changes between two millennium B.C. till the second half of first millennium B.C. What these changes indicate for the Baloch who migrated into Iran around 1200 B.C is not clear; but they may well have involved new religious and mythological conversions as a consequence of cultural permeation on the arrival of peoples from the north, who had greatly contributed toward a settled life and development of material culture in most parts of present Balochistan.

Archaeological discoveries have amply provided the traces of three distinct cultures in Balochistan: First, the Dravidian with great cultural affinities with the Indus Valley Civilization unto perhaps 1800 B.C The second is the Indian, that is, an amalgamation of Vedic and non-Vedic cultures which must have lasted alongside the third major influence that of the Iranians. Antiques found in various parts of Balochistan either have Iranian or Indian imprints. What is important, however, is the constant tribal infusion beginning from 1800 B.C. which had a great impact on the original peoples as well as the newcomers.

There is evidence that Dravidians inhabited the south-eastern part of present Iran and Balochistan. Iranian sources also refer to such kind of people living at Maka or Makkuran.[5] It is somehow established that a few Kushite tribes were settled in Makkuran well before the Creek invasion. There are also faint references in Greek writings and Old Testament of the existence of Kushite race in the east and south. It is also suggested by many historians that various areas of Balochistan are named Kach or Kech after Kush or Kach or Kaj tribes whose Chief was Gandara, after whom the country was called Gedrosia by the Greeks.[6] This cultural infusion was further augmented by different races who ruled the area, and for which we have considerable historical record emanating mostly from Greek historians and some Indian and Iranian sources.

The Greek geographer of the third century B.C, Eratosthenes, has stated that Ariana which embraces a part of Persia and Media, and northern parts of Bactria and Aria was inhabited by Archotoi, Drangian, and Gedrosians who have almost no differences in language.[7] Asoka's inscriptions discovered in Afghanistan have indicated Iranian speaking people who were living in these areas and professed Mazdaism.[8] According to inscription discovered belonging to the reign of Darius I. (522-486 BC), the present day Balochistan, as well as south and south-east Afghanistan, were parts of the Achaemenid Empire. The areas mentioned under Iranian Empire were Gandara (Gedrosia) Maka (Makkuran), Satagush (Sattagydia) and Harahuvatish (Arachosia)[9]

---

5   Yu. V.Gankovsky, Op. Cit. pp.33-35.

6   Thomas Holdich, op.cit, p.35

7   Y.V. Gankovksy, op.cit. pp. 61-62.

8   Ibid.

9   Ibid. p.68

Inter-religious influences

Buddhists or Hindu influences on Baloch religion are fairly visible. In Lasbela and some other areas of Balochistan, the border demarcation signs between Sind and Lasbela were something very strange. These were akin to the various signs on the coins found in Afghanistan and Punjab, and which are generally supposed to be Buddhist emblems.[10] Buddhist imprints have also been found in the caves at Gondrani, north of Bela and Chalgari in Kachchi. In the hills to the west of Bela, there is a sacred place of Hindu worship and pilgrimage at a locality called Hinglag. It is understood to be consecrated to Pārbati, the goddess of nature.[11] The ruler of Lasbela was a Buddhist Priest as late as in the 6th century A.D when Lasbela was part of the kingdom of Sindh.

Archaeological discoveries in other regions of Balochistan give a striking proof of Indian religious impact on the people since time immemorial; and so also on the Baloch who replaced or dominated the original inhabitants. For the religion of indigenous people before the arrival of the Baloch, we must look deeper into Iranian and Indian religions about which there is quite a few historical evidence.

Hinduism,[12] in its present form, is the result of constant historical development and primarily the outcome of Indus Valley civilization and the Vedic culture. There is convincing archaeological evidence showing that the Indus Valley civilization which served as a territorial nucleus for the vast area of the subcontinent with local cultural differences on a minor scale was a close-knit unity, and seems to have embraced a far larger area than the ancient civilizations of Nile and Mesopotamia.

The material available for interpretation of Indian history before the Greek invasion is entirely traditional transmitted orally for many centuries before they were finally reduced to writing. But these are least sufficient for any scientific deductions. The main sources are still the archaeological evidence for the cultural, political and religious

---

10   Charles Masson, op, cit, p.8.

11   Balochistan Though the Ages: A selection from the Government Record, I, op. cit, p.467.

12   Contrary to major world religions, Hinduism is not a definite dogmatic creed but a vast and compex set of religious ideas. It has no fouder, no holy writ, save the literary sources, Rig Veda, the hymns composed over the last two or three centuries of second millennium B.C.

history of India which nevertheless needs scientific scrutiny and objective assessment. The archaeological findings mainly at Mohenjo-Daro and Harappa have provided substantial proof regarding the religion of the Indus civilization. A number of buildings at Mohenjo-Daro have been identified as temples. It is believed that people had beliefs in male and female deities. It is also assumed that there was a great god who had many affiliations, later associated with Hindu god, Siva, and a great Mother who was Great God's spouse and shared the attributes of Siva's wife, Durga-Parvati. Many burials have been discovered which give an indication of the belief of the Indus people in an afterlife. Evidence also exists of some sort of animal cult related particularly to the bull, the buffalo and the tiger; mythological animals include a composite bull-elephant. Some seals suggest influences from, or more appropriately, traits held in common with Mesopotamia.

One thing which should be noticed is that there are definite links on a cultural and religious plane between Indus Valley civilization and Vedic culture. The Vedic and non-Vedic forms of culture were being combined into influencing each other to produce a new cultural pattern. It is difficult to fix a date for such cultural combination and growth, but it can be presumed that it surfaced around 1000 B.C.

The Indo-Aryans adopted the main features of the cult of Siva whose image was identified with that of the Vedic God, Rudra. The main theme of epics written in Sanskrit is connected intimately with pre-Aryan cultural heritage. Brahmi script and numerations may also have descended from the Harapan writing.[13] Excavations in various parts of present Balochistan show a close affinity culturally and religiously with the Indus Valley civilization.

The Aryans who swept through Iran must have brought their own primitive cult with the worship of the natural forces. Their religious practices must have mingled with the native cults to produce Iranian religion which later on developed and refined in the form of Zoroastrianism, in the same manner as the Vedic and non-Vedic cultures in the subcontinent were combined to form Hindu religion and culture. The ancient Iranians were certainly polytheist whose religious belief and practices have close resemblance with other Indo-Iranian and Indo-European groups at the same stage of history[14]

---

13 Yu, V. Gankovsky, op.cit, p 55.

14 The early Irainian religion was polytheism, largely influenced by Babylonian

Zoroastrianism, the great Iranian religion, swept through Iran and its neighborhood as far as Balochistan and parts of present Afghanistan.[15] Probably, during the period when Zoroastrianism was being pushed up to the Indus, the Indian religion, Buddhism, had prevalence in Afghanistan and some parts of Balochistan. Buddhism was in constant contact with Zoroastrianism and later on with Christianity in Central Asia. Buddhist cave figures found in Afghanistan are almost of the same period. *Zend Avesta*, the sacred book of Zoroastrianism, contains several verses which are found in Rig Veda. The Vedic Yama is the Yima of *Zend Avesta*: *Vivasvat* is *Vivagnant*; *Atharva* is *Athornan*, *Asur Maghava* is *Ahura Mazda*. Later Iranian cult Manichaeism had also its impact on the region.[16]

Zoroaster[17] (circa 660-563 BC), the founder of the organized Iranian religion, Zoroastrianism, proclaimed a perpetual conflict between *Asha* and *Druj*, (truth and lie), between *spenta mainya* (the bounteous spirit of good mind) and *Angra Mainya* (the spirit of Evil and confusion).[18] This was further crystallized in the struggle between Ahura Mazda (good mind) and his twin brother, Ahriman (prototype of Devil). The former created good things: light, order, and life and the latter darkness, confusion, and death. The good will attain Heaven and the wicked Hell. Like Judaism, Buddhism, Christianity, and Islam, Zoroastrianism was highly ethical with strong monotheistic

---

mythological practices. Apart from worshipping the force of nature, the Iranian most likely worshipped their ancestors to whose images they attached super natural power.

15   During the Achaemenid period the Medes priests, Magi, had considerably increased their influences in the far -flung areas, which combind with classical Zoroastrianism to produce Iranian religious practices for centuries.

16   Mani vistited Ctesiphon and then proceeded to north-western part of India, present Balochistan in 241 A.D. He preached his religion for nearly a year before his return to Persia.

17   Zoroaser is suppoesd to have been born in Azerbijan in the north-west of Iran. He started preaching first in Khurasan where he got a large number of followers. He is believed to have died around 1100 B.C. There are suggestions that he was born in 660 BC and died in 563 BC,

18   Zoroaster's concept of struggle between good and evil is universal and complete. Man's duty is to serve Ahura Mazda, the embodiment of good and follow the golden rule "to make him who is an enemy, a friend; to make him who is wicked, righteous; and to make him who is ignorant, learned."

elements. It conceived Dualism[19] which sees the entire universe and the world as a dueling ground for the forces of good and evil: God against Satan. The angels against the Devils; the force of light against the force of darkness. It is the religion of salvation which lay in the triumph of the cosmic principle of good over evil. It also believed in the pre-existence of souls[20] that are good by nature.

Avesta, the holy writ which was revised under Sassanid emperors Ardashir and Shahpur II (309-379 A.D.), contains the teaching of Zoroaster. These were unsuccessful endeavors to bring reforms in the Iranian religion.[21]

Mani (214-277 A.D), a native of Babylon, founder of the new religion of Manicheism, tried to combine the doctrine of four great religions: Judaism, Zoroastrianism, Buddhism, and Christianity into his own cult. Manichaeism is also a dualistic religion that postulated salvation through special knowledge of spiritual truth. Mani believed that the soul is a part of God who will not lose interest in the salvation of his own members who will be integrated by God into himself. Through man God saves himself, he is both savior and the one who has been saved: he is 'the saved savior' and in this context, the man is also 'saved savior'.

The Baloch concept of good and evil is very near to Zoroastrian perpetual fight between *Ahura Mazda* and *Ahriman*. Both are equally strong and resolute. The Baloch struggle against evil is a relentless campaign. Baalaach's revenge upon Beebagr on his brother's murder ordinarily appears a common Baloch custom; but viewing in its logical perspective, it is a holy crusade against evil personified in Beebagr. Baalaach sees even the birds on their wings in midnight as his arrows aimed at the enemy: *Aa murg ke shapaan nembaalanth, Baalaache kamaane theeranth,* Doda is noble, virtuous represented

---

19 Judaism, Christianity and Islam considered dualism as a misconception.

20 Zoraastrians considered a corpse unclean and *to be greatly infested by the druj.* To bury or cremate it would pollute the pure elements of earth. The soul is imprisoned in the corrupting substance of the body. Salvation of soul essentially means the emancipation of the soul from its physical prison and its return to its eternal home.

21 Zoroaster denounced the cult of Magi and rejected the pratice of animal sacrifice. He revered fire but never allowed fireworship. Zorastrianism, however, could not save itself from superstitions which crept into it slowly soon after the death of its founder.

by him. Everything emanating from Doda is essentially good while Beebagr and things connected with him, immoral and wicked. Baalaach's killing of enemy cattle and destroying crops reflects the same principle that fight is indefinite, total and universal. He could neither compromise nor surrender. Shey Mureed did not give in after Mir Chaakar married Haani through a stratagem. Mureed is generous, honorable and chivalrous while Chaakar is intriguing and a man of mean character. His fight continues till the last. The interesting point in both the cases is that the force of good symbolized by Doda and Mureed and that of devil incarnate, Beebagr and Chaakar, were engaged in a life-long struggle without any side winning decisively. The Baloch concept of good and evil is deeply influenced by Zoroaster's philosophy. This is more crystallized in folk stories. For all practical purposes, the Baloch is always engaged in combat against forces of evil with an uncompromising determination.

The Baloch often lit fire soon after sighting the first moon of the month which may indicate their respect for the fire which they revered due to their attachment to Iranian religion. He never spat into the fire, and some tribes even swore by the fire.

Influences of Greek culture and civilization on the subcontinent and Balochistan after Alexander's invasion cannot be discounted. The entire culture which blended Greek and Eastern traditions no doubt exercised a tremendous influence on the indigenous peoples of Indian Subcontinent and Central Asia. The peoples of Balochistan also must have got their share of this cultural pressure. According to some traditions, Alexander founded a city at Jau. Greek coins were found near Mastung, Mitadi, Kachchi, and Bela. Greek religious ideas are fully depicted through human forms of Greek deities which had the main idea that the cosmos was basically human. The dreadful monsters, the Hecaton Cheires, Phoncys, the Gorgons, Typhon, Dragons, Gentaurs, Brazen Bulls, Harpies, had contested the Olympians. But in the contest, the monsters were almost always defeated, and the Olympians stood as a defensive bulwark between such monsters and men. The gods surprisingly always preserved a human order.

The Greek mythologies certainly contain some historical truth. For instance the tales of more than one sack of Troy, which are also supported by archaeological evidence, and the labor of Hercules, which fully indicate Mycenaean culture. Heinous offenses such as an attempt to make love to a goddess against her will through deceitful means are also the theme of many legends which reflect the social outlook of the Greeks. Religious myths are mostly concerned with gods and goddesses. They also include cosmological tales of the genesis of gods and the world. Many stories have accounts of the successive struggle of various rulers which culminated in the supremacy of Zeus, the ruling god of Olympia. Another version describes Zeus's love with goddesses and mortal women which resulted in the birth of younger deities. However, such aspects of Greek religious outlook seldom depicted on the Baloch culture.

We cannot altogether discard the Jewish influence on the peoples of the area which must have come during the reign of Cyrus (546-529 B.C.) who adopted a liberal policy towards the Babylonian Jews. But Jewish doctrines might have crept into the area in a much later period through Islam, which was directly influenced by Judaism. Islam[22] successfully attempted to refine the religious and mythological beliefs of Arabia, brought them mostly in conformity with Jewish, Zoroastrianism and Christian philosophies and put them in a more credible form. It had a tremendous impact on the peoples of Central Asia. It was the greatest revolutionary fervor in recent history and had its influence on a significant number of nations throughout the world. The Baloch conversion into Islam began during the time of Caliph Omar, but they were slow in absorbing the tenets of the new faith. According to Al Muqadasi, a tenth-century Arab historian, the Baloch of that period was Muslims only by name,[23] and were less observant in their religious duties.

---

22 Prophet Muhammad (570-632 A.D) founded the Muslim faith at the age of forty (610 A.D.) Very little is known about his early life which is shrouded by legendary tales by his later followers. In the beginning, his mission was purely religious and reformative. His real political career began after Hijra: his migration from Mecaa to Medina, and with this Islam assumed a wider perspective. It came out from its original Arabian character and was proclaimed to be a religion for the entire world. The Prophet's political successes in later years not only changed his religious ideas but his entire political outlook.

23 Al-Muqadasi, Ahsanul Thaqasim, quoted by Dost Muhammad Dost, op.cit. p.363.

Shaping the religious outlook

We have little record regarding the religious and mythological beliefs of the ancient Baloch. However as a section of the migrating Aryan tribes from the Caspian Sea region soon after the first large-scale movement of the Aryan into the subcontinent around 1500 B.C, we can safely presume that the Baloch had the same religious beliefs as those of the early Aryans who had an elaborate pantheon of Devas, the shining ones. Nature was the Aryan's main concern because most Vedic gods were forces of nature. Their method of worship seems to have been the performance of Sacrifices.[24] They were non-vegetarian, and slaying of animals for guests appears to have been widespread and highly praiseworthy.

Aryans had a unique conception of the universe which they believed was peopled by a large variety of celestial beings of different shapes and of varied descriptions. The universe itself was believed to have emerged from nothingness. This view was depicted by the following creation hymn:

> *"Then even nothingness was not nor existence,*
> *There was neither air then nor the heavens beyond it,*
> *Who covered it? Where was it in whose keeping?*
> *Was there then cosmic water,*
> *In the depths unfathomed?*
> *But after all, who knows and how creation happened?*
> *The Gods themselves are later than creation?*
> *So who knows truly whence it has arisen"*[25]

The Aryan religion witnessed great changes after it came into contact with the remnants of Indus Valley civilization whose people appear to have worshipped different deities. The Hindu religion in its present shape, as also the Hindu mythologies, are the amalgamation of Aryan and non- Aryan cultures and religion. After their migration, they settled in the subcontinent and adapted many cultural, religious and mythological views of the indigenous peoples. For instance, the

---

24 The sacrifice appears to be individual as well as collective, involving the entire tribe. The ancient Aryans most probably believed that the universe could be maintained only throuh sacrifices.

25 Rig Veda, tran. A.L. Basham, quoted by Romila Thapar, op. cit, p.45.

Hindu concept of Ahinsa, non-violence, and image worship were clearly non-Vedic adapted by the Aryans through the course of history and established ultimately as an accepted religious norm.

Like other Aryan tribes, the Baloch religious convictions were also influenced when they came into contact with indigenous peoples in Sistan, Kerman, Makkuran and eastern Balochistan. They must have accepted certain religious exhortations primarily from ancient Iranians and later, from Zoroastrianism, Manicheism, and Hinduism.

The Baloch religious attitude is the result of their view regarding the universe. They considered a human being as one of the species having numbered days. He should, therefore, enjoy life, but ostensibly according to fixed principles evolved by their mighty ancestors, because any deviation would be degrading to their great dead and the next generations. It may be presumed, however, that the concept of nature as a totality was perhaps unknown. Only individual natural phenomena such as stars, animals, plants, water, and fire were considered forces that could have immense power to affect human life. These were thus respected and revered.

Sacrifice

The Baloch offered sacrifices [26] on all important occasions including birth, puberty, and death and even on the occasions of construction of houses or before leaving an area and settling in a new place. They sacrificed not only to ward off the evil forces of nature which were believed to be in abundance, but also to please the Divine, and through his pleasure, save themselves.

The nature of sacrifices in ancient time is not known, save the rudimentary idea that the Baloch may have had similar views about this just as the Aryans had before their contact with Indian culture. It appears that though the sacrifice in one form or the other may be prevalent, its present shape must have been through later religious and cultural stimulations. Like most other peoples, the Baloch offered sacrifices regularly on particular days or months till the beginning of the Christian era when their apathy towards religion became visible; or

---

26 Sacrifice is known in all religions as a form of worship. It is a symbolic act aimed at establishing and maintainig relationship of man with the Divine. It had profound significance to individual and to society throughout history.

more precisely, they began to be less observant in their religious duties and adopted somewhat a liberal attitude towards the religion.

They still offer sacrifices on many occasions: in time of impending calamity or danger or before going to battle or after victory. The animal sacrifice is the prevalent form. The sacrifice, or Khairat (almsgivings), in the form of foodstuff or grain or other articles of common use, is also offered. There is no trace of human sacrifice in Baloch culture in any form.[27] Ritualistically, special acts before sacrificing the animal or an object were not uncommon among the Baloch. Most often some kind of prayer was offered, or the animals or objects were formally sacrificed with certain ritualistic saying. Customs prevalent in most societies such as fasting, bathing or seclusion appears to have no place in the Baloch traditions.[28]

It appears that sacrifices were offered at *dour*, or altar, specially selected for the entire community. Blood of the sacrificed animal was to be poured in that place. Sacrifice was also offered of the dearest thing. Beard sacrifices were the most peculiar, that is the beards were cut shorter or shaved. The practice of *Sahbadal*, which means an alternative for life, was prevalent. This involved sacrificing an animal or any other material thing in order to ward off the impending danger to a person suffering from the disease. The origin of this custom is not known.

Veneration of the tribal heroes

The Baloch veneration for his tribal Chief or tribal heroes, apart from being a social and political requirement, has its origin in mythology. He swore by the head of the deceased tribal or family hero or by the head of his father. We have instances in the ancient

---

27 Human sacrifice was prevalent among many peoples. The Greek sacrificial rites addressed to Olympian deities included burning parts of a victim and participating in a cremonious meal offered to the gods. Another rite for Chthonian involved the total burning of a victim in nocturnal ceremonies. Family sacrifices among the Hindus have similar ideas bahind. There are references in Hindu literature of notions of self-sacrifice. Among some anicent peoples, human beings were sacrificed on the occasion of the death of the rulers. Such sacrifices to please the Divine has its curious instace in prophet Abraham's action of sacrificing his son, Isaac, to fulfil a vision.

28 In vedic cult, the sacrificer and his wife were required to undergo an initiation, diska, involing many ritualistic ceremonies before the sacrifice was offered.

history of various peoples where deads were considered mighty and believed to possess supernatural powers. There was a widespread belief among many people about the return of the dead. Stories about ghosts, however, have their place in Baloch folk's tales differing from stories of other peoples only because of cultural or environmental variations.

The belief among the Baloch of the great power of the ancestral spirits was widespread and was perhaps the strongest force for social control and discipline. In social life, they followed certain set principles, and any deviation; he thought, would cause displeasure to their reverenced and mighty deads. Any feast of valor or courageous enterprise would not only renew the past glory but also invoke the pleasure of the spirits of respected heroes. Such heroes had become status symbols, and in a way were the nucleus of many superstitions among the Baloch.

Baloch usually had certain rituals performed in the name of the tribal hero, such as shaving the head of the child for the first time. He always promised or took a vow (koul), to offer sacrifice usually an animal or other objects, at the name of the tribal leader or hero provided he got a child, or a good harvest or good news of his lost relatives, so on and so forth. This is still prevalent but in a different shape. The ancient practice gave way to the custom of going to the shrines of saints for such rites. This is surely a later innovation through Islamic influences.

The priesthood

Another phenomenon was the primitive religious belief connecting religious duties with the office of the Chief (Sardar), which has evidence in Baloch religious and social philosophy. Among the Baloch, the Sardar had no counter-checks by the priest who has been a powerful institution in many societies. This shows that the Baloch Sardar had, perhaps in the earliest times, combined the functions of the priest as well. There are least traces of any religious institution like priesthood[29] separately functioning or influencing the Baloch society

---

29 The priesthood is a cultic organization in all religions. The primary role of the priest wast that of a ritual expert who was supposed to possess special sacred knowledge and techniques of worship. His significance was generally based on alleged deeds and qualities which he possessed and

in any way. Even today, he usually ridicules the Mullah, or clergymen, and considers them dishonest manipulators (One of the meanings of the word Mullah in Balochi is a treacherous and dishonest person). Among some tribes, until recently, the Mullah used to serve, at times, as a personal attendant of the tribal leader who also consulted him on religious issues, but it was the opinion of the chief which prevailed, and usually the Mullah had to give the decree, as the Sardar may have desired, because the Baloch never permitted religious practices to intervene in their affairs or contradict the deep-rooted customs. Consequently, Saintliness which is a quality of moral excellence involving a special relationship with the Divine and which is supposed to have religious perfection is comparatively a recent phenomenon among the Baloch.

The legendary Saints, the line of Kaheeri has been famous. They had their influence on a minor scale since the 15th century. They usually offered their services as arbitrators to negotiate settlement of disputes among the tribal Chiefs. However, the Baloch indifference to such saintly manipulations in politics is evident from the flat refusal of Mir Chaakar to accept the good offices of Shey Kaheeri in the dispute between Rind and Lashaar. Therefore, unlike other societies, the holy men or saints were not a stabilizing factor among the Baloch. Whatever functions he had, he must be a ritual expert, knowing the techniques of worship such as prayers, sacrificial acts, and religious songs.

---

which continued to exert considerable influence even after his death. This is because of the priest's special association with God. From this has developed the modern form of belief in Pir, Kalandar and Buzirg.

Priesthood could be traced to early societies. The Greek hierachic institutions composed of men and women, through whom the Gods were approached and pleased. Priests and priestesses could be found in many place engaging in many specific functions and ritual acts. Among the Baloch, the legendary saints, Kaheeri, are believed to have acquird their names from Kaheer or wild milder tree, on which one of their ancestors mounted as if it were a horse. As a religious sect they claimed to have descended from caliph Omar, a companion of Prohet Muhammad. According to their traditions, they had migrated from Makkuran along with some other Baloch tribes in the late fifteenth century under one of their leaders, Shey Niamat. They are mentioned in Balochi war ballads in connnection with Rind-Lashaar conflict.

In many cultures, religious dress and vestments were sometimes considered necessary and included a wide range of attires, accoutrements, and markings, wore during religious rituals. These were symbolic and used to distinguish the clergymen from others, also to identify ranks within the priesthood. But the Baloch had no rank and file among the clergymen like the various nomenclatures of priests such as Molvi or Mufti; nor did they allow them to be conspicuously distinguished or have greater status than an ordinary person. They had to wear the normal tribal dress and were never allowed to smartly distinguish themselves from the elders or the Chief. It is also evident that generally, the Baloch wore a uniform dress. No identifying marks in the matter of dress are traceable among the early Baloch.

No elaborate structure of religious institutions is visible among the Baloch. Certain personal requirements for a member of a priesthood, such as celibacy which is perhaps the main criteria in Roman Catholicism; and Arcakes of the Digambra sect in Jainism is not traceable among the Baloch. Moreover, asceticism as prevalent in various Buddhist groups, or religious experiences found among some Protestant sects which are the requirement of saintliness, had no place in Baloch religious practices.

Worship

Modes of worship of primitive peoples were varied. The worship of rivers and springs assumed great significance in certain communities. It was believed that indwelling spirits caused the water to move. Many tribes offered sacrifices to water spirits. Some primitive Indian tribes worshipped the spirits of their ancestors. Mother-Earth worship was another phenomenon. Many other non-Aryan Hindu tribes adored mountains. Worship and veneration of objects also depended on various geographical and other factors; the Sun was worshipped in cold regions, while in warmer places the Moon was revered. In certain areas, jungles were revered. The areas covered by jungles where wild beasts posed a threat to human life were worshipped. Wild beast was considered in most societies as the objects of adoration.[30] Polytheistic

---

30 Some Dravidian Hindu tribes worshiped forests and tree spirits. Hindus considerd the Pipal tree sacred, believing that its trunk provided a habitation for Brahma, its twigs for Vusnu and its leaves for other gods.

belief is widely found in all ancient cultures. It received its greatest impetus in ancient Egypt, Mesopotamia, Greece, and Rome. But to say that primitive religion was polytheistic altogether is to discard other significant characteristics of primitive thinking. Belief in some kind of high god, a transcendent being in whom the nature of divinity, in general, is conceptually unified is discernible in the ancient world.[31] A single inclusive concept of god, however, emerged slowly when local requirement gave way to broader national or tribal interests.

The Baloch, nevertheless, had no definite and complex system of worship. It may be due to the fact that the predominant form of religion was never prevalent among them. Ancestor-worship which was practiced among many people did not receive any approval among the Baloch in spite of the fact that they have great reverence for their mighty deads and that the entire society was based on paternal power. Consequently, they never preserved the human remains which were simply interred in the earth. This amply shows that the Baloch veneration of dead was symbolic and their reverence usefully served as a strong influence on a cultural and social plane and as powerful disciplinary force, unlike the Hindus who believe that death is not final but rather one incident in a long series of existence. The Baloch conceived death as a permanent reality. He considered it the most obvious guiding event in human life. But the deads were to be revered because they were the harbingers of unknown existence. They should be in a state of perpetual pride which was possible only if the living members or relatives behaved in a manner which may console his being in the grave. They did not attach any worldly occurrences due to the dead,[32] nor did they accept the idea like the Egyptians that if a man died of violence he becomes an "*ifrit*" (Ghost) and haunts the place of his death.

The Baloch shared the belief with most ancient peoples that the Chief or the ruler generally held supernatural powers.[33] He was

---

31   The real development of monotheism was basically the religious thought of the Jews. They, like most other peoples, had many gods but the belief in one God was asserted again and again through a long line of prohets.

32   Some communities in Africa believed that deads in the underworld cause earthquakes and other disoders. In Mesopotamia and Greece the deads were considerd to be capable of any disastrous action if food was not offered to them. Such beliefs were also prevalent in Chinese and Far Eastern religions.

33   The Sumerians, Egyptians and Persians had similar beliefs about their

considered as the sole protector of his people. Mir Chaakar, Mir Gwahraam, and Mir Naseer Khan were considered having invisible strength.

Burials

The Baloch commemorate their dead on the 4th and 40th day and also annually for a few years. We have little historical evidence to arrive at firm conclusions regarding the exact nature of such ceremonies, but most probably it may be some form of Aryan sacred gathering to bless their ancestors periodically. Rig-Veda records that a sacred beverage, called 'Soma' was set out on the sacred grass, and ancestors were invited to partake of it and bless their descendants. A similar ceremony called "Atheseria" was held in ancient Greece.

The Baloch nevertheless believed in the purity of soul and its existence after death, but there is least evidence that the Baloch believed in the return of the dead,[34] however, the spirit of the deceased

---

rulers who had divine capacity as warriors. Persians came to regard their kings as sacred and therfore it was considered imporper for them to take part personally in wars.

34 Many peoples believed that deads were living in the under world and still effected the life or could be helpful to living beings by persuading the underworld monsters and evil spirits to keep their hands off from them. The Mesopotamians and the Greeks thought that dead were capable of any good or bad actions. They also envisaged an after-life which led to Egyptian building of the temples for the deads. In China, an elaborate ancestor cult flourished, while in India, ancestor worship developed to a great extent. In most civilizations such belief led to construction of tomb not only to protect the body against climatic effects but also to furnish the spirit of the dead with sufficient food, drink and other material needs to ensure its survival. The Hindus considered that death was not final but only one incident in a long series of existence. Archaeological evidences from Indus Valley civilizations also indicate that people had belief in an after-life. Essential articles placed in the grave of the dead show that sush a belief existed. The Iranian religion, Zoroastrianism, considered the body as impure, while the sprit as saved. There were no elaborate arrangements or tombs for the dead. Body was thought to be a corrupting substance in which the soul was imprisoned, and after that the body to be disposed of in such a mannor that the possibility of polluting the finer elements of water or fire could be avoided. However, in most civilizations, the dead could not affect

may be living and affecting individuals. The mighty dead expected the living people to behave in a particular manner. Any deviation from the accepted norm was considered improper. It was against his sense of honor to have any shameful effect of the living man's action on the spirit of his departed ancestors. Among the early Baloch, dead were simply buried without constructing any tomb or building on their graves.[35] There are also no indications of preserving the body of the dead or supplying them with the foodstuff. Food offering to them or *murdagaani shaam* (dinner of the dead) was practiced among the Baloch in a much later period mainly through Middle Eastern and lately Islamic superstitions. Dinner of the dead is celebrated as a feast in which the favorite dishes of the dead from a family are prepared and distributed as almsgiving. No arrangements were made for identification of each grave save those of tribal heroes. Headstones were erected on the grave of important people. Sometimes it was covered outwardly by small stones.

In folk stories, we have many instances regarding the return of the spirit of the dead; but unlike Hindu belief, it never existed again in another shape or body or came as the Egyptian "Ifrit" Dead spirits, however, appears in dreams, approving or disapproving certain steps taken or contemplated to be taken by a living relative. Such appearances occurred often by night to the elderly person of the family.

Burial was done in the daytime and seldom at night. Not only evil spirits may cause some inconvenience to the body at night but it was not thought proper to dispose of the dead at night. If the death occurred at night or when it became impossible to bury it immediately, the body was buried the next day. It was placed in some spacious place in the house surrounded by close relatives and friends who kept awake the whole night. Persons whose bodies might be damaged at the battlefield or lost and eaten by beasts, the remains of their bodies

---

the worldly life. The Greeks thought death (Thonatos) is the twin brother of sleep (Hypnos) and this spread the view that death is merely a sleeping state in the passage from this life to an afterlife.

35 At Nichara, east of Kalat, corpses were discovered in a few caves which were still preserved but later pulverized on being touched or exposed. Similar corpses were found in Mashkhel and Hanidan in Lasbela district in common graves. They must be well before the Baloch migration to these areas. The interesting aspect of Nichara corpses was that they were found in hill caves and not in regular graves or tombs.

were buried with usual ceremonies according to circumstances. Bodies of the hated criminals or social outlaws were interred mostly without ceremonies.

Khairat (Almsgivings) was offered on the occasion of death. This must have its genesis from the Baloch observation of certain rites periodically for the spirit of their ancestors. Its present form must have been influenced by alien cultures. Construction of tombs or decorating the grave of a Saint has crept into the Baloch culture in a later period mostly through Islamic practices.

Monsters, fairies, jinn

Ancient peoples believed in the existence of an intangible or spiritual being who was interpreted as soul, ghost, ancestor spirit, ogres, and monsters or simply as other objects. Stories about superhuman creatures were also universal. Fairies or their counterparts appear in the literature of many peoples. In many societies, calamities were considered the working of supernatural forces. Sometimes, such creatures were believed to be helpful to human beings. Belief in evil spirits was another innovation to this superstition. The Baloch never doubted in the existence of such supernatural beings. Folk stories have a large number of such references where they are either helpful or harmful according to circumstances. Belief in them was widespread, which was further augmented by Islam.[36]

The Baloch believed that Jinns are fiery bodies who are intelligent and imperceptible. They are capable of appearing in various shapes and colors. Found mostly in deserts and jungles, they are also attached to sorcerers (*Jaathu*). The Jinn could be harmful but be controlled to the benefit of the individual. It could cause harm to women, children or persons of any age, or cause such persons to go out of their minds unless cured by a Mullah or *Shey*. What the Baloch did to ward off the influence of Jinn is not exactly known. Probably, they restored to some

---

36 The Islamic concept of Satan which is slighlty different from jinni in its very essence, was not unfamiliar among the Baloch. In Zoroastrianism, there is a constant fight between the forces of good and evil. In Islam, Satan is the power that opposes god in the heart of man, that is, the Devil fighting good. The idea of Satan in Islam is obviously borrowed from Judaism and Zoroastrianism.

superstitious methods (exorcism) to force the withdrawal of the Jinn which could not be seen or heard by ordinary persons, while it could listen and see human beings. They were believed to be of both sexes and having ugly outlooks and repulsive bad odors. Their feet were believed to be hoofed.

There were widespread notions regarding Jinn in various stories and in so-called personal anecdotes narrated by many people and widely believed. It was believed that demons, good or bad, could be living anywhere especially in isolated places, and any person who may have a chance to visit those places of their inhabitation could be harmed. They thought that supernatural creatures were everywhere in the universe, in the seas, the sky, the plains, valleys, mountains, jungles, and deserts. The underworld was inhabited by invisible creatures, good as well as bad who may affect human affairs.

In Baloch folk stories, Jinn fall in love with women. They consort with humans under certain conditions. They were helpful or harmful to people according to circumstances. Womenfolk were particularly afraid of Jinn who could possess her forever until some person (exorcist) with extraordinary magical or spiritual power causes its withdrawal. Another interesting phenomenon is about the language of the jinn or demons. They can speak any language, but surprisingly, in the majority of cases, they always speak a foreign tongue. When a person was possessed by a Jinn, he/she usually spoke a language which was not Balochi. The Jinn who would speak through his/her victim did not know any other language. The alien language spoken by the victim was mostly Persian in western Balochistan; Hindi or Sanskrit in the areas adjacent to the Indian subcontinent, and of late a few words in Arabic. Majority of the magical formulations or phrases used by exorcists were also in alien languages or Balochi mixed with some alien words.

Sorcery

The concept of an evil spirit, or to a lesser extent, jinn and ghosts, found its extended rationale in the widespread belief in sorcery. It was the human enduring mental and physical strength which made it possible to acquire tremendous spiritual strength that could enable someone to control the evil spirit and employing them to the individual's advantage. The act of sorcery depended on verbal formulations and magical strength of words, which were considered most important. The Baloch thought that such formulations or words (abracadabra) were fixed and had specified strength. The precepts would be effective only when enchanted or repeated in a fixed manner in an isolated place, preferably in a remote graveyard after midnight. It was said that evil spirits were usually at work at a particular time of night and could harm the reciter of magical phrases if he showed a little sign of mental and spiritual weakness. This practice was continued according to the magical effect one wanted to derive. If unharmed, the individual would acquire the control of some evil spirits which would serve him as a guard and an evil agent who could bring disaster to anyone desired by his master.

There appears to be a wide difference between what was said to be illicit sorcery (sehr), and white magic, enunciated by Islam. The former was prevalent in Central Asia and India. Magic in orthodox Islam is worked by obeying Allah, bringing adjurations by Allah to bear on the spirits. Islam traces all white magic back to Biblical King, Solomon (ruled 970- 931 B.C) who was given the command of the legions of Satan and jinn who worked at his will. He had unusual wisdom and insight, and knowledge too great to be measured. Solomon spoke of trees and plants, talks about animals, bird, reptiles, and fish.[37] He had esoteric powers. Forces of nature were at his disposal. According to Muslim legends Soloman had great power of magic, divination, and wisdom.

The words (abracadabra) said to have magical effect had apparently no meaning. They are, if etymologically analyzed, either Balochi words reconstructed to an apparent meaningless form or predominantly of Sanskrit origin. For instance, the following spells for snake and scorpion bite and hysteria, obtained by the author from Miya Azeen, resident of Nodezz, District Kech, seem to be quite meaningless in form and structure:

Lankaasa kod samandarse, utarpichou harbanduhu, peergue mijirkhim. Each beech, lade pade; thumhaari zaatka, thumhaari atela; chapeela chapaala; charnuka guruka; Mahdi karesh. koule Selemaan ben-Daaoud; zabardusth And Jarusam jakaana deersam, manukan ashashan zabadan anboh.

---

37 I King 4, 29-33.

However, later formulations included Persian, Arabic and other sources which can not be identified. These words absolutely have no meaning but to be the mode of action and a strong expression of human will and urge of human desire into words directly aimed at invoking the forces of nature beyond ordinary comprehension.

Sorcerers were feared by the Baloch who believed that they possessed extraordinary destructive powers through evil agents. Such agents at the command of sorcerers could inspire love or hatred, avert impending disasters, guard anyone against the enemy, and could easily harm the opponents. The sorcerers were asked to derive omen, or *paal*, for securing wishes. The sorcerers usually did not engage in normal economic or social endeavors.

The Baloch associated certain animals with sorcerers. They thought that the animal spirit could be bound up to that of the sorcerer who could assume an animal form or any other shape he liked. The sorcerer or *Jaathu* perhaps always rode the hyena or sometimes the hog.[38] They rode their opposite sex and believed to have intercourse with the animal. A sorcerer or *Jaathu* believed to rode the hyena (*apthaar*). They could travel hundreds of mile in a short period. Another innovation of Baloch conviction was that the sorcerer or *Jaathu* usually ate human "heart", by first dislocating it and then pulling it out from the human body. This was perhaps one of his most feared actions. He or she mostly attempted to eat the heart of a sick person. When a *Jaathu* so desired, he or she first caused illness and then attempted a pull out of the heart. The method usually applied was to call the name of the person late at night; and when he or she inadvertently replied back, the magical effect would be constructed. The affected person was immediately taken to illness and subsequently died due to pulling out of his heart. Surprisingly, however, the sorcerer could never attempt to cause harm to the tribal chief who was always considered not prone to such things.

---

38 A contrasting allusion could be made to burak described in Muslim traditions as a mare with a woman's head and a peacock's tail. Prophet Muhammad is belived to have ridden this animal on the night of ascension, Miraj. The animal was said to have been brought by Arch-angel, Gabrael, for Prophet Muhammad and took him first to Jerusalem and then to the Heavens. According to Al-Tabari, a similar animal was used by Prophet Abraham to pay periodic visits to his son, Ismael.

The Baloch believed that the witches or magicians have their periodical gatherings where extraordinary feasts were performed and observed by them. There are many instances of such gatherings of Jinn or witches in Balochi folk stories.

The Baloch believed that persons having magical powers could secure a strayed cattle from the wild animals during night or day. The magical effect called, *"ampaas"* literally meaning protection, could be constructed and wolves or other beasts could not eat the un-shepherd or strayed animals in the jungle. The similar verbal formulation could cause a man's sexual impotency or render a weapon effectless.

Although, having supernatural powers, however, if a *Jaathu* was apprehended and a portion of the hair or one of her or his teeth was cut, the magical power on the affected person was believed to come to an end, and the victim was relieved from evil consequences. The *Jaathu* would also lose the magical power until acquired after going once again through the entire process of witchcraft.

The belief in sorcery was an affirmation of human control of supernatural force through spirit agencies and compulsive power of words. It employed symbols, images, and idols for individual manipulation and interests. The Baloch belief in the power of spoken words may have perhaps its roots in the ancient belief that words or formulations persistently repeated will invariably bring a response. This is also the basic idea in religious prayers, the forms of which by their phraseology alone are mostly command. It is held that they will bring the desired results. The Baloch magical traditions appear to be of Aryan origin with considerable variations necessitated perhaps due to changes in circumstances. In Rig Veda, there were strong utterances of incantations and spells, charms and witchcraft, hymns to inanimate things, devils and demons. The primary conviction in sorcery, however, must have been strengthened when Baloch came into contact with other peoples in Iran and further east in present Balochistan. He had a somewhat strange faith in magic and alchemy. Belief in the charm of robbers to lull the house people, or cause their sleep: to prevent any misery to individual male or female and charm to expel diseases were widely held.

Dreams

This is a primitive belief that dreams predict the future. The Chester Beatty Payrus is a record of Egyptian dream interpretations dating from 1991-1876 B.C. In the Iliad, Agamemnon is visited in a dream by Zeus messenger prescribing his actions. The Indian Atharvaveda, a fifth century B.C. document, contains a chapter on dream omens. Archaeological discoveries in Nineveh included a dream –guide from the Emperor Ashurbanipal's (668- 627 B.C.) library.

The controversy regarding the correctness of dreams has been a major point in all civilizations. Dreams have never been accepted as always accurate. In Odyssey, dreams are classified as false and true. In the Bible, Joseph interpreted sheaves of grain, the moon, and stars as symbols of himself and his brethren. The Old Testament is full of prophetic dreams; those of Pharaohs, Joseph and Jacob are particularly striking. In many cultures, dreams were invariably considered true. Some Indian people identified dreams with reality and often pursued a course prescribed directly or as implied by the dreams. In general, however, social interpretations of dreams were varied with differing effects on social structure.

Dreams were a peculiar phenomenon and an extreme curiosity for Baloch whose mind had always been preoccupied with monsters and superhuman beings who lived in dangerous lands far from human reach and usually appear in nightmares. As the monsters were good as well as bad, the dreams must have certain indications: either good or bad for the individual. The Baloch believed in dreams. Their close ethnic relatives, Kurds, after dreaming something valuable expected to get that by all means including the use of force because they thought that the dream must have its rationale. What was, however, peculiarly interesting is the fact that not all the dreams of ordinary men were considered significant which might have required exposition especially on the matters of collective importance. The individual dream may be of some relevance regarding oneself. But matters of common importance such as war, calamities or matters having some impact on the tribe, must have been dreamt by the tribal elders and the chiefs who immediately called for interpreters, and in some cases, proper precaution was taken. Certain matters implied in the dreams were kept a secret, while others could be explained in public.

In folk stories, dreams and their definitions have great relevance and are the theme of numerous stories whose main character usually dream something valuable and set to achieve it or try to avert dangers after dreaming. The Baloch even considered offering sacrifice usually the only appropriate measures to ward off dangers after having dreamt to that effect.

Superstitions

The Baloch believed that certain happenings on the earth were the result of stars or some other heavenly agents. The changes in the location of certain stars in certain periods of the year were the subject of their forecast regarding social, economic problems of their people.[39] Rain or calamities could be forecast by the keen observers of stars. They considered sun or moon eclipses as bad omens and offered sacrifices on these occasions.[40] As the Baloch regarded these heavenly bodies with sanctity, they considered such eclipses to be the result of some extraordinary happenings brought about by some deep conflicts. Therefore the impact on humans was inevitable. During such eclipses, the pregnant women were neither allowed to see the eclipse nor were they required to move for fear of the bad impact on the child in the womb.

Many customs among the Baloch had some vagarious concepts behind them. For instance, some tribes, instead of offering rain prayers, which is still in vogue in some communities in the contemporary world, a naked or semi-naked woman plowed the fields at night all alone. This they thought would cause rain. Another practice was that the youths selected amongst themselves one or two persons who were made up in a particular way and painted to look very ugly. Then the boy was taken to each house saying *Kalaan Kambaro* and begged for foodstuff from the residents. These foodstuffs were

---

39 Most people in Persia and India believed that a bear who was a giant or an animal of great strenght held the earth up, and when changing position, earthquakes could be caused.

40 Belief concerning sun or moon eclipses are very anceint. Most people interpreted such eclipses as battle or dying of the one of the two heavenly bodies. It has been viewed with deep concern among many peoples. Some defined eclipses as the love-making of sun and moon.

taken along with the boy to an isolated place outside the settlements and cooked while the boy himself would be kept away during the cooking and eating process. Similarly, girls would make a doll and carry it through the tents saying *Shishalaan shaalo thrampoke aap de.*

What is interesting among the Baloch is that iron or anything made of iron such as sword or dagger had some impact on jinn or other evil forces. Mother still never forgets to have a knife below the pillow of a newly born baby. On the first night of the marriage, a sword or knife was quite essential to ward off any evil spirit.[41] Women drew a cross (+) called *Rakk*, literally meaning protection on the walls or on some other conspicuous places in the house. Sometimes *Rakk* were drawn on a baby's pendulum *(Gwanzag)*. A straight line on the forehead of the newborn was made to protect him or her from evil forces. Tattooing on young faces of women was also common. All these have clear mythological origin having some similarity with the signs found through archaeological findings from Gedrosia belonging to the latter half of the 1st millennium B.C.

The Baloch considered certain animals, such as sheep or cows as virtuous. Lizard and Garter snake *(dehkaan–mar)* was never killed out of respect. Among plants, the fig tree was considered sacred. It was believed that if one could obtain fig flower and put it in anything, the quantity of that thing would increase two-fold.

The typical style of Balochi beards must have its genesis in mythology. It was perhaps the most peculiar make-up which had hardly any parallel. Style of beards could be changed if somebody in the family died or some calamities betook the tribes. Balochi embroidery *(doch)*, has clear imprints closely related to Vedic culture. Similarly, two unshaved tufts of hair *(bull)*, were left while shaving the child's head. This also has some mythological context belonging to the Aryan period. Identical pictures have been found with similar haircuts during excavations in Balochistan.

The Baloch men wearing *durr* (earrings) must invariably have some mythological origin apart from decorative purposes. The womenfolk's *durr* (large golden earrings) of specified style and embroidery on clothing now regarded purely decorative has its roots in mythological

---

41 Defloration of the bridegroom by the priest or the chief was prevalent among many people in the Far East. They believed that great danger was attendant upon the first intercourse. Ritualistic coitus was aimed to ward off evil from the husband and also from the wife.

imprints. Apart from the above, the following superstitions are still in vogue among various Baloch tribes:

1. A person ready for a journey or has just started it if called from behind, was always considered inauspicious. In such a case he would discontinue his journey because it was feared that the purpose of the journey would not be met. Journey on Fridays and in some places on Wednesdays was never regarded proper. Among some tribes journeys towards the east or west, whatever the case may be, on particular days were considered inappropriate.

2. Neighbors usually refused a request for the salt after sunset till next morning.

3. It was believed that a woman in the first quarter of her pregnancy (*the period of nepagaan*), if not given eatables she desired, such as an apple, a roasted bird or a particular dish of her choice, the child in her womb, would be either born premature or with some deformity.

4. During military movements for an attack on the enemy, if a hare or a black cat ran ahead of the army (*Lashkar*) or crossed it, it was considered a bad day for combat. For an individual on the journey if a hare crossed his path he would return and restart it.

5. *Kiyaanch*, a small bird, owl or *boum*, were considered vicious, while a hog, swine or wild pig (*ladi*) was also bad perhaps due to Islamic influences. *Simurg*,[42] an immortal mythical bird like the Egyptian phoenix was said to be of good omen.

6. Women never took a bath on Saturday which falls on the 16th of a month because it was considered inauspicious for her brother and father.[43]

7. Certain days were not considered good for marriage or a wedding ceremony.

---

42 Most probably, Simurg has crept into Baloch myths through persian influence. It appears to be the same as phoenix in the Egyptian mythologies which after living for nearly five or six centuries in Arabian desert consumed itself in fire, rising renewed from the ashes to start another long life. Simurg in folk stories is an immortal and a very powerful bird which may help human in time of need under certain circumstances.

43 Shambeh o Shaanzdah sar mashoud brathaani gwahaar,
Shambeh pa bratha shar naenth shaanzdah pa petha.

8. The Baloch drew auguries from various things: the hiss of a serpent, or the flight direction of a particular bird on a particular occasion.

9. The Baloch used to put a pot full of water in a deserted place, especially in the mountains. It was believed that the water if drank by birds, would become sacred: and then if given to infants, they could understand the language of the birds.

10. A light bluish stone, *Peroza* or light blue beryl, could help ward off evil eye; it was also hung around the neck to heal tonsil infections.

11. A sign on a certain scapular bone (*burdasth*) of goat or sheep, was seen to draw omens and forecast the future.

12. The Baloch drew omen from the leaves of Mideterrean dwarf palm *(pish)*. It was called *maasag*. A few leaves of *pish* were put together and then set apart. The expert on this would forecast present or future happenings.

13. *Espanthaan* or peganum harmala seeds were set on fire as incense to set up smokes in the house on particular occasions to ward off evils.

14. The Baloch never spit into fire or towards the sky.

15. *Momenai*, (mineral pitch or mineral wax) a tar-like substance obtained from mountains, considered sacred and heal body pain.

16. When the Bride was taken to bed during the first night of the marriage, she carried cotton seeds in one hand and grains in the other. Before sitting on the bed, she would throw these beneath the bed. This was done for bringing prosperity to the family.

17. Among some tribes, it was considered inauspicious for the mother-in-law to meet the bridegroom for three days after the marriage.

18. After a child was born a woolen band made of goat hair, was tied around the bed of the mother, a similar band was put like a bracelet on the right hand and right foot of the husband. Sometimes a few cotton seed were also put in some hidden places in the house. Leaves of *karag* (Calotropis gigantea) with white flowers were put in a few places in the house to ward off evil forces.

19. A pregnant woman would avoid visiting another who might be having child-pain. Similarly, a woman having her menses would not visit a woman who has just delivered a baby.

20. If someone, especially a child became the victim of "evil eye" a cup was filled with water, and leaves of *pish* were rounded on the head

of the child many times after putting them in that water. This is called *"Nazarburri"* and repeated for a few days. The water was then poured outside the house in the morning and evenings at least for three days. It was believed that this would have a healing effect on the victim of "evil eye".

21. If there is an epidemic in a herd of goats or sheep, one of the animals died of that disease was buried at the gate of the *waad* (a wooden compound prepared for the animals) and others were driven out over the buried body of the dead animal. It was believed that the disease which was caused by some evil forces would end. Similarly, to save the cow or bull from *rikk*, a diarrheal inflection, a red cloth was fixed at the tail of the animal.

22. Among some tribes, women never started making new clothes on Tuesdays. It was believed that clothes prepared on this day would have a short life and would catch fire not long after.

The Baloch religious and mythological beliefs in their recent forms are the results of great cultural changes since their movement from the Caspian Sea region. First, they came into contact with indigenous ideas. The Iranian religion, Zoroastrianism and Manichaeism had their influences; so also Judaism and Christianity, and Islam, in a much later period. One of the major reli.

gious impacts was of Indus Valley Civilization which was further refined through the Aryan amalgamation to be perfected in the form of Vedic religion. All these factors had a great role in shaping the Baloch religious and mythological outlook. Islam, the latest organized religion of Arabian origin which was imposed on the Central Asian peoples beginning from seventh century A.D. also had its impact. The Baloch was one of the earliest peoples in Central Asia to convert to the new faith. But surprisingly, they were never religious fanatics, nor were they regular observers of religious duties. The deep and vigorous conflict between the centuries-old socio-religious traditions and the new faith was perhaps intense and the Baloch evolved a moderate line between the two. They did not give up their ancient ideas altogether but adopted certain customs which were the requirements of the new faith. This balancing factor is still there among the Baloch. They are largely Sunni Muslims except for a small segment who later converted to the Zigri sect of Muhammad Junpuri in the sixteenth century

A.D.[44] Some of the Baloch tribes in Western Balochistan and Sindh became Shia perhaps for political compulsions. Other religious sects in recent history are quite insignificant and have least influences on the Baloch religious outlook.[45]

There appears to be a considerable modification in Baloch outlook regarding religion in recent decades. The Baloch, like many people, were religious having their rituals and sacrifices, but their perceptions regarding religions were changed because of their persecution by the powerful rulers in the name of religion beginning from the genocide acts of Sassanid emperors Anusherwan and Shahpur which continued up to the Safavid dynasty in Iran. The intolerance among the followers of powerful religions of the region and persecution of members of one group by another made them almost skeptical about all ranges of religious approach. Secondly, Islam, which has been variedly interpreted mostly to meet the requirements of socio-political changes in the 6th century Arabia, was sometimes viewed by the Baloch as a threat to their national identity and culture. The diagonally contradictory interpretations and formulations of religious injunctions by the *Ulemas* (Islamic religious leaders) of divergent schools of thought also contributed toward Baloch antagonistic attitude. Even today, in Pakistan, and recently in Iran, the incessant cry of Islam is being raised with fanatic intensity to safeguard the interests, other than purely religious, at the cost of what the Baloch consider their legitimate national rights.

The Baloch reaction has been very sharp and penetrating and resulted in a general dislike of religion. The only instance of religious

---

44 Zigri, a religious sect of Indian origin, had its followers in western Balochistan most probably since the early sixteenth century. From evidences available, it appears that the sect was founded by one Muhammad (1442-1505 A.D.) of Daapur in Junpur, India, who was expelled from there due to his religious beliefs. He travelled to Kandahar and Farah. According to Zigri traditions, from Farah, he disappeard and after some times, made his way to Persia and finally took his abode on Kohe Murad, two miles from Turbat, in southern Balochistan. He preached his faith to the people of the area who became his followers. Nevertheless, the person who took abode at Kohe Muraad may be one of the followers or a descendant of the Muhammad Junpuri.

45 Rafais and Biadhiahs, two religious sects of the coastal area, Gwadar, now almost extinct, have their orgin in later eighteenth century. They are considered to be among the various sects of Islam.

intolerance in the entire Baloch history was the personal attitude of Mir Naseer Khan, the Khan of Kalat, towards the Zigri sect of Muslims whom he considered heretics. His hostility towards them was a political overture for gaining the control of southern Balochistan which was exclusively following the Zigri doctrine, however, never appreciated by the common Baloch.

Unlike their Pakistani, Iranian or Afghan neighbors, the Baloch were never incited in the name of religion. On the other hand, they always promptly responded to the call in the name of their culture and traditions. In recent history, when the subcontinent was divided and Pakistan was created in 1947, there were gruesome murders and wholesale massacres in various areas in the name of religion. Muslims killed Hindus in a wild frenzy of religious fanaticism. Hindus also retaliated against the Muslims. But there was absolute communal calm in Balochistan, except for Quetta where Pakhtoons created some trouble for the Hindus. The Baloch never harmed neither the non-Muslims nor looted or damaged their property. They treated members of other religious groups with due respect and opposed those who wanted to spread hatred among various peoples. Still recently, when Shiaism was re-established in Iran after the downfall of the Shah, Muhammad Raza Pahlavi; and when the majority of Iranians were swept away by religious fanaticism, the Baloch in that country disliked this obstinate bigotry.

FIVE

POLITICAL STRUCTURE

The Baloch political system was entirely based on tribalism whose internal structure or the primary organization remained unaltered throughout the ages, save some insignificant variations necessitated due to political, military and socio-economic developments. Tribalism was further cemented with family and clan organization.

Kinship which had its characteristic in clan and family structure also played an important role. It was a major factor in regulating and systemizing the individual behavior which in turn influenced the formation and sustenance of socio-political organization of the entire tribe. The nature of political association was by no means religious. The whole population was a centralized political unit headed by the tribal Chief with considerable authority and prestige.

The tribal system was founded on the principle of decentralization of power. The heads of the section and sub-sections enjoyed sufficient power and were independent in managing the affairs of their sections, except matters concerning war and peace. They adjudicated minor disputes and acted as the court of appeal for their people.

For the individual, the tribal system served as a practical means of enhancing one's good fortune in the economic field and a position of respect in other matters. The main characteristic of the system was that it treated every member with due regard and accorded him an honorable place in society. In the Baloch tribal society, no one could tolerate a secondary or indignified position. Every Baloch had the same privileges and rights as enjoyed by the Sardar or elder. He never forfeited his identity as an equal partner in all matters in social life. Basically, everything circled around the individual, who was extremely proud and mindful of his exalted position. He was rigid in his social outlook and hardly charmed by alien customs. The individual member of the society was to maintain the true spirit of Baloch character and behavior.

The Tribal unions

The political, economic and social nucleus of the early Baloch was the tribe; the association of the various tribes may have taken firm roots at a later stage of history when it became impossible for one tribe to face the challenge from hostile forces. It must have taken a definite shape, though very rudimentary, in the beginning, soon after the Baloch migration from their original home. Their fight against indigenous peoples of Eastern Iran and ultimately the present Balochistan may have established the feelings of greater unity among various tribes. The Baloch and the Kurds must have had some tribal alliance of their own. The Baloch resistance to Anushervan's army was not a single tribal fight or concern but all the tribes fought the aggressor. As a matter of fact, it was the foreign aggression which had greatly helped in developing the Baloch united approach, and more appropriately strengthening the tribal bond, at least in times of grave national crises. However, the developed form of the tribal fraternity was witnessed first in the sixth century A.D. against Anushervan; three hundred years later against Kerman ruler, and subsequently during the Rind Lashaar conflict. On the first two occasions, they unitedly fought the Iranian authorities; and in the later, most tribes engaged in warfare on either Rind or Lashaar side. In Western Balochistan, various tribal unions were formed during Safavid and Qachar rule; however, the fight could not be sustained and their resistance against these Iranian dynasties was ineffective. The Kalat tribal or national confederacy was the zenith of tribal integration and harmony in the Baloch history. The efforts of Mir Dost Muhammad Barakzai to unite the tribes and rulers (Hakim) of various regions in order to strengthen the Bampur state in the early 20th century failed due to various external and internal factors.

The tribal organization

The tribe was generally constituted from a number of kindred groups. It had many sub-divisions or clans who claimed to have blood relations with one another through some ancestors. Such groups generally occupied a specific territory and managed their affairs independently under a local headman subordinate to the Chief of the tribe or Sardar but used his powers through general consent. He decided matters concerning his people. He was responsible to the Chief. The Sardar had powers over the sectional heads that were responsible for carrying out the policy guidelines formulated by him with the approval of the council of elders. There was, however, a sort of mutual dependence between the Sardar and sectional heads and among various sections. The headmen had the support of the Sardar because they had the corporate will and understanding of their respective people behind them. But that support could hardly be invoked or utilized against the Chief who had the general mandate and support of the entire tribe. The Chief, theoretically, had control over the headmen though he was always depending on them in many matters.

It was more convenient for the administration of the tribe that local leaders were invested with authority. Generally, the tribe was scattered over a vast area, and it could have become a practical impossibility for the Chief to have all the administrative and judicial powers centralized in his own hands. However, the tribal sections were not authorized to declare war or come to peace with any other tribe without the consent of the Sardar or the council of elders.

The tribal organization was a loose Confederacy of various classes and groups who could hardly be homogenous. Outsiders from all quarters were admitted in the tribe. If a sub-section of a tribe migrated to another area or had its quarrel with its Chief it declared itself no more attached to the main tribe and asked for the membership of another tribe, first as an ally: and when it proved its worth by rendering meritorious services to the tribal cause, as a full member of the new tribe. In that case, it would lose its original tribal name and identity and became the part of the new one with all privileges, including a share in tribal land and membership in the council of elders.

In times of danger, the entire tribe would be united to meet the challenge. Normally, gathering of the tribesmen as a body or assembly was rare. Majority of the people, however, participated in selecting the Chief; on the birth of a son to the Chief or some similar occasions, but only in an extraordinary situation the entire tribe would gather to hear their elders. In normal conditions, all decisions were taken by the headmen or the tribal council.

The people could replace their headman on the charges of his dubious character, gross irregularities or misuse of power. His incompetency in wars or other emergencies also provided sufficient cause for his replacement. In such an eventuality, the people, especially the elders of the section, gathered and voted to remove him and selected another head for that section. It was not necessary for the new head to have been related to the former.

The Sardar had many checks on his authority. He was answerable to the people. He had to take into considerations the wishes of the masses. Decisions of the council of elders were binding. All important decisions were to be passed by the council. The Sardar had only one vote. He had, nevertheless, a great influence on his council, and generally, his opinion prevailed. This also depended on the personality and general reputation of the Chief. All important policy matters were put to vote. Any member of the council could put a point to be considered for discussion in a meeting. The common folk had the vested right to appear before the council and argue a matter concerning him or of general interest. However, the right to put forward a matter of general interest was generally exercised by the sectional headman who was the member of the council. In the case of differences of opinion among the members, the Sardar could adjourn the meeting and reconvene it after due consultations amongst the delegates. In case the differences persisted, the Sardar could use his prerogative power and announce a decision provided it was inevitable because of some emergency. The decision of the council did not have to be unanimous. A majority of votes was, however, required for a decision. Normally, issues concerning the relationship with other tribes were decided unanimously. In that respect, the Sardar was the main source of guidance, whose words were taken for granted. But matters concerning the tribe or dispute among its various sections required considerable consultations and judicious settlement because any wrong step could alienate an important section of the tribe who would migrate to a remote area or throw off allegiance from the main tribe. This was, however, restored to in extreme cases and was very uncommon.

The Sardar

The Sardari was the executive branch of the tribal organization, while the Sardar was the Executive Chief. It was essentially a very useful institution catering to the administrative, judicial, economic and social requirements of the people in the ancient and medieval epochs. Unlike most of the ancient monarchies and some of the Asiatic principalities in medieval times where there was no limit to the power of the ruler, the Baloch Chief had considerable checks on his authority. There was no statute law to guide governmental machinery. The guiding factor was the Baloch code of conduct and traditions which had a stronger influence than any law prevalent in any contemporary society. The Sardar could not act contrary to tribal principles evolved throughout centuries. He was answerable in his action not only to the council which was the custodian of tribal code and which the Sardar followed in his public as well as his private life but to every member of the tribe. He was the symbol and most revered figure among the people. The Sardar was considered to have been bestowed with mystic qualities. He was a political as well a moral leader. He had no regular force of his own to enforce law and order. The entire tribe was behind him. He was obeyed in all matters. Nobody could contemplate any disobedience to him as long as he acted judiciously and according to traditions, nor could he be conceived to behave in a manner inappropriate to his exalted position. He was sympathetic, considerate, philosophical and virtuous. He was honest, austere, well mannered, judicious and brave.

The Sardari institution remained undiluted for centuries till the modern era when the Baloch came under the British overlordship in the second quarter of the nineteenth century. As a part of its concerted plan to perpetuate its rule in this vitally strategic area,[1] the British

---

1 Balochistan which was always regarded strategically vital got added importance in 18th and 19th centuries when Great Braitain and Russia contested each other in Central Asia. Napolean's invasion of Egypt and his contemplated attack on India through Persia brought Britain, Russia and France to far-reaching foreign policy decisions. However, the French defeat

Government began to systematically deface the entire socio-political structure. The Sardars who were always the best representatives of the people were compelled to take sides with the alien rulers against the interests of their masses. The Judicial system was corrupted and manipulated. A wedge was drawn between the people and their Sardars who became the paid agents of the British masters. Even after the departure of the British, the new rulers from Punjab followed the same strategy in Balochistan. The majority of sardars who are selfish and hypocrites were imposed on the people by the rulers in order to maintain the so-called Sardari system in a cruel and hated form.

The office of the Sardar was not hereditary; it was an elective position which required great personal qualities for the man who held it. Not only the head of the tribal sub-sections and divisions participated in the election but the Electoral College practically consisted of all important individuals in the tribe.[2] They were guided

---

and the disintegration of Napolean Empire in the beginning of the 19th century left Britain and Russia as the only contesting powers in the region. The British authorities in India wanted that Russia should be confined up to the Oxus which was considerd the natural border between the British Empire and Russia which however, considered itself always vulnerable from Asia and kept extending its influenece along its border regions. Its eastern frontiers could be strengghened by establishing friendly governments in Kabul and Tehran and by taming the border tribes. The strategic attraction of pushing the Russian influence farther east and getting warm water ports for its trade and expanding navy in the Indian ocean region, and especially the Persian Gulf, had been another strong element in Russian foreign policy approaches. Great Britain formulated its socalled 'forward policy' keeping in view the strategic importance of Balochistan and the extreme limits of Sistan as a formidable factor in what was then termed as the Indian frontier question. While Britain wanted a presence in Afghtaistan, it wished a complete sway in Balochistan and Quetta as a strong British military outpost overlooking Kandahar and Kabul. The Great Game against Russia was marked by a sustained hostility between the two powers throughout 19th century. Protracted negotiation and the British unsuccessful adveture in Afghanistan resulted in a more logical approach toward Afghanistan which was ultimately accepted as a buffer-zone between Russia and British India, to the advantage of Great Britain. The Russian apparently accepted British suzerainty in Balochistan and its influence over southern Persia.

2   Tribes or sections considered by the Baloch as their inferiors and who were aligned with them, however, did not take part in the election of the tribal Chief.

in their decisions by the council already in existence. There were no hard and fast rules regarding the succession of a new Chief. The succession issue was decided according to circumstances. Generally, the eldest son of the Sardar was elected as new Chief, but in case he was of inferior social status from his mother's side, the question of his election would become the point of much dispute.[3] As the Baloch considered the purity of blood essential for the leader, they never agreed if their Sardar descended from inferior stock.[4] The Chief had generally several wives and also had issues from slave girls or low-caste women and concubines (*sureath*), sons from such women could never to elect as Sardars. Usually, the succession had to be smooth and without a difference. But if serious differences cropped up the matter was put for active consent or vote, and the majority decision had to be accepted. In such a situation there were a lot of maneuvering and behind-the-scene manipulations from various quarters. The chiefs of neighboring tribes discreetly intervened in some way or the other to ensure the election of a favorable candidate or person of their choice as the new Chief. If the Sardar died without a male issue, a suitable person from the closely related family of the former Chief or some other noble family was elected.

The election ceremonies were simple. A *paag* or turban was put on the head of the elected person as the Sardar, and he was formally declared the leader. This ceremony was performed by a representative of the council of elders; and in later stages in history, this act may have been performed by some religious personalities. There was no other ceremony because the tribe theoretically was still mourning the death of the departed Chief. Ceremonies were generally postponed till after a considerable time when succession was formally celebrated with much

---

3   According to some tradition, Mir Chaakar was the son of Mir Shaihakk from a low caste mother. He was elected Sardar in the life time of his father because Shaihakk feared that after his death, the tribesmen may oppose Chaakar's candidacy. The Baloch stilll consider most of his later actions as Sardar as not behoving a true Baloch. Mir Chaakar's conspiratorial mind is said to be hereditary from his mother's side.

4   The caste consciousness still prevails among the Baloch who could hardly accept a person socially inferior to be elected as their leader or representative. In the modern era, quite a few persons who had a chanced breakthrough in the politial field, were not successful because they were not accepted by the Baloch masses. The main reason was the strange approach towards their racial impurity.

rejoicing including music and dancing. All important people from the tribe took part in the ceremonies. Nevertheless, among the ancient Baloch, there is no evidence of any ceremonies on such occasion which was quite simple.

If there were no differences on the question of succession, the ceremony was held within three days, and the eldest son was elected the new Chief. In that case, the election had to be confirmed by all the headmen, later on. If the Sardar proved incompetent and did not come up to the trust reposed in him, he could have been removed from the office through a vote of No-Confidence from the council. In that case, the opponents had to prove a strong case of corruption, moral degradation or incompetency as a result of mental or physical illness or disease. An overwhelming majority of tribal subheads and important persons had to vote to form a resounding majority demanding his dismissal. However, a vote of no confidence was rare except in extraordinary circumstances. In case the Sardar did not accept the majority decision, they would be united under some elders or the new Chief, if elected by then, to fight the ousted leader. Mir Mahaabath Khan (1733-1736 A.D), the Khan of Kalat was deposed by the Baloch Sardars after a confrontation in Kalat. They made Iltiaz Khan (1733-1736 A.D) their new Chief. But his dictatorial attitude was resented by the sardars and he was ultimately deposed, and Mahaabath Khan was once again declared as the Khan.

The Council

The tribal council composed of the heads of clans and sub-clans was the supreme body dealing with administrative, judicial and other important matters affecting the welfare and general condition of the tribe. Each clan had its own council of elders to decide matters concerning that section.

Issues were decided mostly through general consent, often unanimously, but if there were differences of opinion on any particular matter, majority decision would prevail. As regards membership of the council, practically all persons of consequence and heads of the clans were members. Their election to that position of clan heads was almost identical to that of the Sardar, but their nomination or subsequent membership in the council was subject to the confirmation by the Chief which was always forthcoming. Generally, the Sardar would exert pressure in many ways to get a person of his own choice elected as head of that section, and ultimately, as a council member. Membership of any person could be challenged. The Sardar with the approval of the council could replace any member. In such an eventuality, the person would lose his position as the local head of the clan and be replaced through a general consensus or election. The method of election for the Sardar or the clan head was identical, that was the formal expression of trust which was general and explicit. Normally heads of clans were counted: those who favored and those who opposed.

The council was convened usually on important issues. The disputes of less importance were decided by the Sardar himself. On certain occasions, very important decisions were taken by the Chief and subsequently put before the council for its consent. In case the Chief did not convene the council or he was prejudiced against a party or was himself a party to the dispute, the council members after consultation amongst themselves could convene the council and decide the matter without the Sardar presiding or attending. In case of differences of opinion, there was a standstill and the action on the issue was postponed. In the case of unanimity, the Sardar had to accept the decision.

The council was the most important institution of the entire tribal structure. It was in its developed form before the British hegemony in Balochistan. The most important institution in the Khanate dealing with local government was practically the council. Even the Khanate in its administrative set-up was the prototype of the tribal council.

Economic system

The most important characteristic of the tribal society was that no class or group of people was denied access to the resources of nature. Every tribesman had the freedom and vested right to exploit the natural resources. The system at the beginning appears to have been one of joint economic responsibility of the community. The cultivation of land was given to a group of people, and the produce was distributed equally according to requirements. At a later stage, however, various tribes held lands for cultivation and grazing purposes and such distribution was less judicious and depended upon the relative strength of the tribe. Powerful tribes occupied fertile lands; tribes of lesser consequence were contented with less fertile areas. This often led to tribal rivalry and conflict in a series of un-ending tribal wars. The Rind Lashaar conflict in the 15th century was basically over the fertile lands of Gandawa. Gohar's affair was, nevertheless, one of the immediate causes of the thirty years conflict, but the cardinal point in that fraternal war was for political hegemony and economic reasons.

There were no regular taxes apart from contributions among the tribesmen in times of need or tribal emergency. As there was no administrative infrastructure, a bureaucracy, a regular army or a peacekeeping agency to be paid, there was no need for taxes. Commerce and manufactures were also tax-free. However, at a much later stage, taxes became a feature in economic life. The foreign rulers imposed taxes which were always resented and refused. In Kalat confederacy, taxes were imposed on a few items. The major item of tax was the land produce. There was no taxation on cattle and other private belongings.

Lands were usually jointly cultivated. Sometimes private possession of the land acquired by individuals or groups was recognized but that was always subservient to the right and obligations of kinship and other interests. This was also a later practice. Theoretically, however, rights on land were vested in the community and not in any individual. In later times, communal ownership was reduced and it was taken by the people with the same lineage. The lands were afterward re-allocated to meet the claims of the individuals and groups belonging to the original community. All other economic resources were also regarded as jointly owned. Private ownership was largely confined to cattle, weapons of war, utensils, and ornaments.

As the entire administration of the tribe rested on the shoulders of Sardar, seasonal contributions were made towards the Sardar under various nomenclatures to meet his personal and family expenses. He was allocated a certain portion of land to cultivate for his own use. Such property was held by the Chief by virtue of his title. In case he was removed from his position, the land was restored to the tribal pool for reapportioning to his successor.

Military system

The striking character of the tribal organization was that it was basically a close-knit unit of fighting men. The Sardars had no regular army.[5] All the able-bodied men constituted the fighting force. During the brief conflict between Mir Naseer Khan and Ahmad Shah Durrani, the Khan rejected the initial peace overtures by Ahmed Shah and sent him a register with a list of about two hundred and fifty thousand men ready to take up arms against the Afghans. During the reign of Mir Mahmud Khan 1, a register of 250,000 troops was maintained which appears to be the entire strength of his subordinate tribes who were obliged to provide men in time of war. There was no regular army on that scale. The Khanate force was a collective army divided into three main territorial divisions with separate distinctive banners. Men from Kach Gandawa, Kalat and Noshki were red-flagged; the troops from Sarawaan used a green flag, while forces from Jahlawaan used yellow color. Mir Chaakar has been mentioned in Baloch traditions as having had forty thousand Rind and Mir Gwahraam thirty thousand Lashaar fighters. Neither the Khanate nor Mir Chaakar or Mir Gwahraam ever deployed in any single combat even a portion of the men mentioned being under arms.

The tribal fighting force received no pay. However, they were entitled to get a share of the war spoils, distribution of which considerably differed from time to time. But it is evident that Sardars and other heads got a greater share. Of late, the persons who possess a particular type of arms or performed specific acts during the war had a specified share in the war booty. Shares of a horseman and of a footman differed; so was the difference for war spoils of a person carrying bow and arrows and sword.

Although the entire tribe, men and women, were supposed to be up in arms when required, the Baloch seldom met in the battlefield tribe-to-tribe or in full strength. A considerable number of men headed either by the Sardar or the next man in the tribal hierarchy contested the enemy. Surprise raids were rare, but in a series of continuous battles, such raids were not discounted when both sides were practically at war.

---

5   Mir Naseer Khan and his successors had a small standing army which was merely symbolic and was constituted primarilly of housebold servants.

Men were generally commanded by the sectional heads who were under the overall leadership of the Chief. War codes included movement during particular hours and analysis of intelligence reports. The war was not the business of any particular section of the people or tribe but every Baloch had the obligation to place his services for the battle.

Judicial system

The Baloch had given justice the highest place. He would never tolerate injustice in individual or collective life. The over-riding judicial philosophy was the principle of revenge and compensation. System of retaliatory justice had the strongest roots. He considered it his duty and inalienable right to do himself justice by compensating the property lost or by avenging the blood of his relative. He was always reluctant to transfer this right to any person or body of persons to exercise it on his behalf. It was always lawful and honorable for him to avenge his injuries in the same proportion as he had received. Certain results of retaliatory justice were continuous strifes and killing lasting for generations.

The council of elders could adjudicate the cases where both parties agreed to accept the decision. However, once they consented to the council decision, it was then binding. The decision was arrived at after considerable discussions on the merit of the case. As every Baloch was truthful and considered it a dishonor to tell a lie, there was no difficulty in ascertaining the facts of the issue. Both the parties to the dispute or their representatives were allowed to argue. Witnesses were called whenever required. When the case concerned two sections of the same tribe, they were represented by their respective heads in the council. Non-compliance of the decisions could invoke serious punishment, usually fine and in certain circumstances even outlawry. Nobody had the strength and courage to refuse to comply with the decisions which had the moral and physical strength of the entire tribe behind. The persons found guilty of a crime against the tribe, such as treason or rebellion, could be severely punished. The punishment could be death.

Although the council had no absolute authority, it nevertheless, had inherent powers when the offender's act had a bearing on the entire tribe or might have resulted in general discontentment among the people or imminent bloodshed among various sections of the tribe. It was always guided by tribal codes and precedents. There was virtually no deviation from the general principles of justice to all, regardless of one's position.

The Baloch political system revolved around the Sardari system and served as the institution which offered individual freedom to a Baloch as long as his personal interests did not contradict the interests of the community as a whole. Before the occupation of Balochistan by the British in 1839, Sardars were elected among the best of the individuals in a tribe. In a way, the Baloch political system under tribalism was a form of meritocracy. Formation of tribal unions was important for the survival of the Baloch against the onslaught of powerful forces and ultimately manifested itself in the establishment of the first Baloch state of Kalat in medieval times. The phenomenon of Meid was the Baloch way of diffusing tension between individuals, groups, and tribes.

EPILOGUE

Taking into consideration the linguistic, cultural, historical and geographical factors, it has now been established that the Baloch belonged to those tribes who spoke Indo-European languages. There are strong indications that they were among those Aryan tribes who began their migration three thousand years ago from central Asia.

For the origin and etymology of the name Baloch, many guesswork can be found in the related historical documents. Some put it as a derivative from Median Brza- Vaciya from brza-vak, loud cry, in contrast to namravak, quite polite way of talking while others maintained that Baloch is made of two Sanskrit words, Bal (strength) and och (high or magnificent). Another line of etymology is suggestive of Baloch as a nickname meaning a "cock's comb". Recently, the new theory has been postulated for the etymology of the word 'Baloch'. The Baloch being the modified or deformed form of Balaschik who was a national entity and inhabitants of the region of Balashakan or Balashagan during the Achaemenid period.

In medieval times, the Baloch were generally referred by Arab and Persian writers as Koch o Baloch. Both are considered to be one people, with two names being synonymous except for the difference of language.

From linguistic evidence, it appears that the Baloch migrated eastward from the region of the Caspian Sea, a theory borne out by the clear relationship amongst Balochi, Persian, and Kurdish. Balochi descends from ancient Iranian dialects dominant in the territory of Media and Parthia. It is this consideration that furnishes one of the major arguments in support of the proposition that the areas adjacent to the northwestern coasts of the Caspian were the original Baloch homeland. Of the movement of the Baloch south-eastwards from northwestern areas of Iran we possibly find evidence in the parallel

165

between the Baloch and Iranian languages of Farsi and Khuri to the south of the Dasht-e-Kabir, a parallel which stems from the prolonged existence of Baloch tribes in the area.

Balochi derives neither from Parthian nor from Middle Persian: the original source is sometimes held to be a lost language which must, however, have a certain affinity with Parthian or Middle Persian. Balochi has a pronounced individuality which is greatly influenced by Median speech and the Kurdish dialects. It occupies a distinct position among all the Iranian languages, resembling most other Iranian tongues in showing a nearer relationship to ancient Avesta than to old Persian.

The ancient vocabulary, the breakdown of sounds, grammatical structure, forms of inflection and pattern of reconstruction of such form are the factors usually analyzed to establish any relationship among various languages. Mere loan-word which has crept into a language as a result of contacts with the speakers of other tongues cannot be the proper criterion for determining language kinship. Normally, there are three main sources of word entering Balochi: foreign words such as English or Arabic, the latter through religious influence; words derived from neighboring languages such as Persian, Pashtu, or indigenous languages such as Jadgaali, Saraiki or quite recently Urdu; and words coined from original Balochi courses to meet modern Scientific and technological requirements. Another interchange of words occurred in Balochi due to the frequent change of speech among the many linguistically separated Baloch and Brahui clans. Many Baloch tribes speak Brahui, while people from the Brahui tribes speak Balochi. Moreover, almost all the Brahui tribes in Iranian Balochistan now speak Balochi. Sometimes it becomes difficult to assert with certainty whether there is a Brahui substratum in Balochi or whether it is Brahui that has been influenced by Balochi. It is, however, probable that Balochi had some influence and that the original Dravidian phonetical system of Brahui has been adapted to that of its Balochi neighbor.

However, some time in ancient history, the Baloch or some of the Baloch tribes might have been subjects of the Semitic Chaldean Empire. The Babylonian or Chaldean empire extended from the mouth of the Euphrates-Tigris to Euxine, the river Halys and Palestine, parts of eastern Iran and the southern shores of the Persian Gulf. The empire comprised of many peoples- including Hamites,

Semites, Ethiopians, and Aramaeans. These peoples spoke various Semitic languages, prominent among them Chaldean, Aramaean, Hebrew, and the Syriac and Turanian dialects with Ethiopian or Kushite vocabulary. The Baloch connection with Chaldea comes with reference to Asiatic Ethiopians, of whom physical comparison has been made to some people in ancient Balochistan well before the arrival of the Baloch. Two possible theories have been put forward. Firstly, the Chaldean Kushite or Asian Ethiopians might have spread east and west, on the one hand to Susiana, Persia proper, Karmania, Gedrosia and India; and on the other hand, a second proposition is that the Cushites might have colonized the coastal region of Arabia and from there spread to Makkuran, Kerman and areas bordering India.

The Asiatic Ethiopians who constituted one of the major races of Chaldea obviously are not the Baloch of today. They may have a certain relationship with the peoples inhabiting ancient Balochistan, but the Baloch settlements in Gedrosia by all accounts date from centuries later than the referred Asiatic Cush. However, the physical description of the Asiatic Cush fits many people in the subcontinent and Balochistan. As regards their affinity with the Baloch, the description could apply to a great extent to indigenous Balochized Darzaadag factions in Balochistan. A critical study of Baloch hereditary characteristics, physical features, socio-cultural and religious traditions amply demonstrates the Baloch racial kinship with Aryans and reveals the Caspian Sea region as their original homeland.

It appears that from the northwestern Caspian region, or from the region of Balashakan, as now being postulated, the circumstances forced the Baloch to migrate *en masse* towards eastern regions of the Iranian plateau in a series of migrations most probably beginning during Sassanid period. During the 7th century, there was a significant presence of the Baloch tribes in Kerman and Sistan.

The Baloch appear to have been in constant conflict with mighty forces throughout history. The first organized attack on them on a large scale came from the Persian monarch Khusraw I, the Anushervan (531-578 AD), around 531 AD. According to Arab historians, they also fought bloody battles against Arab invaders after the invent of Islam. Muslim rulers of Iran also fought to keep the Baloch under control in order to keep the trade routes open through their territories and also keep the Baloch influence in their areas to a minimum.

The genocide acts against the Baloch by various Iranian dynasties after the collapse of Arab rule in Iran and the incursion of Turkic tribes in Sistan and Kerman caused a wave of migrations of the Baloch tribes from these areas further east and south. It was the period when Makuran and Turan regions of present-day Balochistan came under the linguistic and cultural domination of the Baloch. Their migrations eastward and southward may also have been the result of the Seljuk invasion in the eleventh century and the devastating inroads later by Genghis Khan during the 13th century. By the 14th century, the new wave of migrating Baloch tried to settle in the central Balochistan up to the Jahlawaan hills, where they came into conflict with a group of Brahui speaking Baloch tribes who had arrived and settled there in an earlier migration. The migration further east into the Indus valley and Punjab took place at a much later date.

Balochi which is spoken by the majority people in the Pakistani, Irani and Afghani part of Balochistan is not homogeneous. The people of various regions speak their own variety of dialects with an overriding influence from neighboring tongues. It can be divided into three main dialects of Eastern, Western and Rakhshani with their respective subdialects. The subdialects may include Kalati and Sarhaddi. It also includes dialects of the Marv region. In central Balochistan, the region dominated by the Brahui speaking tribes, the people are mostly bi-lingual, speaking Brahui along with Balochi. Balochi has been influenced by the Indo-Aryan languages such as Sindhi, Punjabi and a variety of other tongues such as Saraiki to the east and Pashtu on the north, with Persian influence on the west can easily be observed.

Folktales and poetry have been the vehicle of the dissemination of the Baloch history and socio-political traditions. Poetry is still one of the main sources. Being unwritten, however, its authenticity with regard to many events sometimes becomes doubtful. Most of the poems must invariably have been edited throughout history and many of them have been lost. The Poetry which has come to us takes the form of epics, lyrics, lullabies, fables, and riddles, knitting together ancient traditions, customs, legends, proverbs, religion-mythological beliefs and cultural traits of the people. The Baloch epics can be compared in forcefulness and lucidity and for their content of prudential sayings with Greek and Hindu epics. They depict a pastoral and nomadic culture of a proud and warrior people. Balochi poetry is not merely an arrangement of words and phrases devoured of any purposefulness or indifferent to geo-social and political happenings, it undoubtedly shows a great amount of poetic imagination and artistry. It depicts the culture and tradition of the people in vigorous, simple and a very appropriate manner. These poems appear to have been constructed either by the individuals involved in wars or romance or the court poets of various tribes, called Zangi Shahi.

Baloch society places immense importance on the individual and accords him an honorable status. Consequently, he is highly egoistic and deeply proud. *Kay mani gahgeerien sara guddieth?*—who can cut off my majestic head?" is a true manifestation of the Baloch attitude. He disdains intermarriages with social inferiors. Among the Baloch all people were noble, enjoying equal social status. However, the indigenous peoples who could not claim equality with Baloch were employed as workers or peasants.

It was an open society where men and women work in unison. The Baloch give women privileges which to a great extent are identical to the equal social rights advocated in the ancient Iranian religious work *Din Kard*. The Society was organized on patriarchal lines with the formal authority vested in the males, who were primarily the holders and inheritors of property; though the woman does inherit and manage the property and also plays an important role in managing family affairs. Polygamy was practiced but divorce was rare.

Baloch society was based on the concept of mutual benefit and loss. The political, economic and social nucleus was the tribe, whose structure was firm and permanent for the good of every member. The tribe was organized mainly on the Aryan pattern and therefore, was a self-sufficient political, social, economic and cultural unit, headed by the tribal chief, who enjoyed considerable authority. The post of the chief was not hereditary. The tribe was constituted from a number of kindred groups but form a closely knit unit of fighting men, ready to defend individual and tribal interests. Every individual had equal access to natural resources and a vested right to exploit them, in a system based on common economic responsibility. The land was jointly cultivated by groups of tribesmen or clans. Private possession of lands was clearly a later phenomenon. The tribal organization and its external structure have been witnessing transformation mainly through external socio-economic and political influences but without any mark or dramatic effect on the existing social conditions.

The Baloch cultural traditions were based on moral principles of good conduct beneficial to the entire people. Such traditions were acquired by the individual through a constant process. He was brought up in a specific social environment where he was taught to respect the rules sanctified by society. He was never insulting. Even punishments meted out to criminals were never degrading. There was never hanging or maiming or blinding, which were prevalent among many peoples neighboring the Baloch. The honorable way of the beheading was always used to kill a criminal.

The Baloch was truthful and honest. Telling lies was considered an insult. He would keep his word at any cost: once he vowed to do something, he would do it by whatever means in total disregard of the consequences. The woman's dishonor was washed off only by blood. Prostitution, abhorred as a vitiating act of perversion and highly intolerable, was punished with death.

The Baloch had a penetrating sense of individual and collective justice. He considered it his duty and inalienable right to take revenge. The right to do himself justice was never delegated to others. Once a wrong was committed the wrongdoer was bound to pay in the same coin. Sometimes the revenge is taken even after generations. He who does wrong was symbolized as evil while those taking revenge were thought noble and virtuous and virtue was to overwhelm the evil.

The Baloch always sides with the oppressed because he has a just cause. The tradition of *Baahot* (Giving asylum or protection) in all its theoretical aspects was to help the weak. He would withstand hardship and suffering in defense of the oppressed who have sought help. Defending a person or his interests when he sought help was by no means helping the wrong side. Basically, it was the weak and oppressed who used to request help and such help was always forthcoming.

The Baloch respected the brave while despising the coward. He had great regard for the fallen hero, even belonging to the enemy, whom he buried with full honors. Enemy leaders were neither ridiculed nor belittled, even if defeated. In the Baloch epics, heroes from both sides are equally praised for their bravery and courage. This attitude was evident during the Rind-Lashaar conflict and tribal wars of the medieval period. These principles were upheld even in individual conflicts. Baalaach, a folk hero who avenges his brother's death by fighting an entire tribe single-handedly, respects Beebagr, who killed his brother. Conceptually, he considers him evil incarnate and vows to fight to the last, but he praises him for his skilled use of the sword. In another folk story, a mother, while mourning the death of her fallen son in the hands of a young foe, profusely praises the enemy for his courage and bravery, boasting that her son was killed not by a scoundrel but by a brave and honorable youth.

The Baloch hated the enemy from the core of his heart but had the greatest regard for those whom he felt considerate towards him. He was frank and deeply affectionate. Once obliged, he remembers it for life. *"Thaase aap ware sad saala wapa bedaar"* -you should have affection for the person for a century who once offered you a glass of water, so goes the saying.

Religion has always been a part of human intellectual behavior but the Baloch can truly be called to have been secular if the term is appropriate to denote a people who have not allowed religion to overwhelm their traditions and socio-economic beliefs. We cannot trace Baloch religious thinking in ancient epochs, apart from the fact that their religious view was very much closer to the Aryans and they generally belonged to the religious fraternity of the Central Asian peoples, especially the Iranians. The Baloch religious ideas perfected throughout centuries and which must be a fine amalgam of Iranian and Indian religious views. The earliest reference regarding the Baloch secular approach during medieval times was found in the Arab historical accounts. They referred to Baloch as Muslims only by name never observing the tenets of the new faith, Islam. Surprisingly, the Arab faith, in spite of the crude political force behind it, could not diffuse throughout the Baloch society. Pre-Islamic thinking was still prominent among the bulk of the people. The Baloch's religious outlook is still not shaped entirely by his acceptance of Islam more than fourteen hundred years ago.

Although Mullah or Pir has a role in countering the evil of jinn, monsters or any supernatural affliction, there was no established clergy or priesthood, nor did Pir or the so-called religious celebrities exist among the Baloch. The Baloch considered the religion as purely a personal affair. Their attitude towards religious matters was one of the philosophical calm. Any attempt on the part of the Mullah to transgress reasonable limits was strictly resisted and his influence other than religious rites and ceremonies was curiously limited. After their conversion to Islam, a Baloch was neither Sunni nor Shia, he was simply a Baloch first and a Muslim next. The Zigris among the Baloch, which is one of the numerous Muslim sects were never discriminated against (In recent decades, the ignoble attempts by certain Mullah enjoying the active support and connivance of the ruling faction in Pakistan to create bitterness among the Baloch by importing sectarian feelings from elsewhere, miserably failed to attract the people who generally regarded the entire game as an attempt by the Pakistan rulers to divide the Baloch masses).

The Baloch although not religious, nevertheless, superstitious. He drew auguries from almost everything or happening which may be slightly unusual. The cry of the wild beast, the sight of a serpent or of a certain bird in the early morning or at night, a hare crossing his path when he starts on a journey; and a host of other happenings were sufficient for him to perceive things auspicious or inauspicious for him or for the entire tribe. He had certain days considered unpromising for a journey or for ceremonies such as marriage. Sorcery also played an important role. The sorcerer or *Jaathu* was the most feared person and his evil influence could be lessened by a shey or Mullah. The Baloch belief in Jinn or fairies or monsters was overwhelming.

Evolved from an agro-pasturalist background, and from the sufferings of centuries during there wanderings in Iranian Plateau, the Baloch socio-cultural traditions center on preserving their national identity and individual independence which was nurtured by tribal set-up. These might be some of the factors which helped the Baloch to retain its identity as a distinct people despite the assimilating endeavors of powerful states that had dominated the Baloch throughout its tortuous and painful history.

REFERENCES AND BIBLIOGRAPHY

Abisaab, R. (2003) <u>Converting Persia: Religion and Power in the Safavid Empire</u>. New York: I.B. Tauris.

Adontz, N. (1970) <u>Armenia in the Period of Justinian</u>. Translated by N. G. Garsoïan. Lisbon: Calouste Gulbenkian Foundation.

Anderson, B. (1991) <u>Imagined Communities: Reflections on the Origin and Spread of Nationalism</u>. London and New York: Verso.

Arberry, A.J. (1953) <u>The Legacy of Persia</u> (edited). London: Oxford Printing Press

Arfa, Hassan (1968) <u>The Kurds: A Historical and political study</u>. London: Oxford Press.

Arrian, L. F. Xenophus. (1958) <u>The Campaigns of Alexander</u>. Translated by Aubrey de Sélincourt. London: Penguin Classics.

Bachmann (1977) <u>Afghanistan- from Darius to Amanullah</u>. Lahore: Orient publishers, 1977, p.25.

Baladhuri, Ahmad ibn Jabir. (1924) <u>The Origins of the Islamic State</u> (Kitab Futuh Al-buldan). Translated by Francis Clark Murgotten. New York: Francis Clark Mugotten.

Baloch, Muhammad Sardar Khan (1958) <u>History of Baloch Race and Balochistan</u>. Karachi: Pakistan Press

Baloch, Muhammad Sardar Khan (1965) <u>The Great Baloch</u>. Quetta: Balochi Academy

Baloch, Muhammad Sardar Khan (1977) <u>A Literary History of Balochis</u>, Vol, 1 Quetta: Balochi Academy

Begum, Gull Badan (1974) <u>Humayun Nama</u>. Trans. Annette S. Beveridge, Lahore: Sang-e- Meel Publication

Bellow, H.W (1977) <u>An inquiry into the Ethnography of Afghanistan</u>. Karachi: Indus Publication, 1977, p 20.

Bellow, H.W (1978) <u>Afghanistan –Country and People</u>. Lahore: Orient Publishers, 1978, P. 25.

Bergen, Evan (1972) <u>Dictionary of Mythology</u>. New York: Dell Publishing company

Bongard-Levin, G. M. (1980) <u>The Origins of Aryans: From Scythis to India</u>. Translated from Russian by Dr. Harish C. Gupta. New Delhi: Arnold-Heinemann Publishers.

Bray, Denys (1977) <u>The life History of a Brahui</u>, Karachi: Royal Book Company

Bray, Denys (1978) <u>The Brahui language</u> Vol, II Quetta: Academy, pp35-36

Burnes, Alexander (1975) <u>Travel into Bukhara and a Voyage on the Indus</u> vol Karachi: Oxford University Press, 1975, pp 162-164

Childe, V. G. (1926) <u>The Aryans: A Study of Indo-European Origins</u>. London: Kegan Paul.

Curzon, G. (1966) <u>Persia and the Persian Question</u>. London: Frank-Cass & Co.

Dashti, N (2012) <u>The Baloch and Balochistan: from the beginning to the fall of the Baloch state</u>. Trafford Publishing

Dashti, N (2017) <u>The Baloch conflict with Iran and Pakistan: aspects of a national liberation struggle</u>. Trafford Publishing

Dashti, N. (2008) <u>The Cultural Context of Health</u>. Quetta: Balochi Academy.

David, N. (1996) <u>Sassanian Armies: The Iranian Empire Early 3rd to Mid-7th Centuries AD</u>. Stockport, UK: Montvert.

Dost Muhammad Dost (1975) <u>The languages and Race of Afghanistan</u>. Kabul: Pashtu Academy, 1975 p 362.

Dye, James W. & Forthman, Willian H (1967) <u>Religions of the world</u>. New York: Appleton Century Crofts

Elfenbein, J.H (1966) "The Balochi Language- A Dialectology with text. <u>Royal Asiatic Society Monographs</u>, Vol, XXVii: London, 1966 P.10

Elphinstone, Mount Stuart (1974) <u>The Kingdom of Caubul</u>. Vol I London: Karachi, 1974, pp,205-207.

Encyclopedia Britannica: Vol 8,p 908

Ferrier, J.P (1979) <u>A Caravan Journey and Wandering in Persia, Afghanistan, and Balochistan</u>. Karachi: Oxford Printing Press, 1979, PP 432 -435.

Firdausi, A. (1908) <u>The Shahnama</u>. Translation by Warner and Warner. London: Kegan Paul, pp. 33–34.

Frye, R. (1961) "<u>Remarks on Baluchi History</u>." Central Asiatic Journal, Vol. 6, pp. 44–50.

Frye, R. (1983) "<u>The Political History of Iran under the Sassanians</u>." In Ehsan Yarshater (ed.), Cambridge History of Iran, Vol. 3, No. 1. London: Cambridge University Press, pp. 116–181.

Frye, R. (1984) <u>The History of Ancient Iran</u>. Vol. 3, No. 7. London: Beck.

Gankovsky, Yu. V (1971) <u>The peoples of Pakistan</u>. Moscow: Nauka

Ghirshman, R (1978<u>) Iran-From the Earliest Time to the Islamic Conquest</u>. London: Penguin Books

Griffiths, John C (1981) <u>Afghanistan-Key to a continent</u>. London: Andre Deutch1981,p. 13.

Henriques, Fernando (1962) <u>Prostitution and Society-A survey</u>. London: Macgibbon & Kee

Hewsen, R. H. (2001) <u>Armenia: A Historical Atlas</u>. Chicago, IL: University of Chicago Press.

Holdich, Thomas (1977) <u>The Gates of India, Being a Historical Narrative</u>, Quetta: Goshae Adab

Bhabha, Homi (1990) <u>Nation and narration</u>. London: Routledge

Hooks, S.H (1963) <u>Middle Eastern mythology</u>. London: Hazell Watson& Vinery Limited

Imperial Gazetteer of India, provincial series, Balochistan. Calcutta,1908, reprinted: orient Publishers, Lahore, 1976, pp21-22

Istakhri, Ibrahim ibn Muḥammad. (1961) <u>Masalik al-mamalik</u> (in Persian). Tehran: Bungah-i Tarjumah va Nashr-i Kitab.

J.L Myres (1918) <u>The Dawn of History</u>. London: Williams and Norgate

Janmahmad (1989) <u>Essays on Baloch National Struggle in Pakistan: Emergence, Dimensions, Repercussions</u>. Quetta: Gosha e Adab.

Khan, Ahmed Yar (1972) <u>Mukhtaser Tarikh-e-Baloch aur Khawanine-e-Baloch</u>. Quetta: Aiwan Kalat, pp 7-8.

Kuz'mina, E. E. (2007) <u>Origin of the Indo-Iranians</u>. Brill: Leiden and Boston.

Levy, Reuben (1918) <u>The Social Structure of Islam</u>. London: Cambridge University Press

Maqaddesi, A. (1906) <u>Ahsan at-taqasim</u>. Translated by M. J. de George. Leiden: Damas.

Mari, Mir Khuda Bakhsh (1974) <u>Searchlights on Baloches and Balochistan</u>. Karachi: Royal Book Company

Masson, Charles (1976) <u>Narrative of a journey to Kalat</u>, (First published London, 1843) Karachi: Indus publication

Masudi, Abu al-Hasan Ali. (1989) <u>The Meadows of Gold: The Abbasids</u>. Translated by Paul Lunde and Caroline Stone. London and New York: Kegan Paul.

Myres J.L (1918)<u>The Dawn of History</u> London: Williams and Norgate, 1918 P. 128.

Naseer, Gul Khan (1979) <u>Balochi Razmia Shairi</u>, Quetta: Balochi Academy, p.14

Oliver, Edward (1977) <u>Across the Border, Pathan and Baloch</u>, (First Publish, Chapman and Hall, London 1890) Lahore: Al Biruni

Purohit Swami (1973) <u>The Geeta</u>. (Translation). London: Faber and Faber Limited

Rawlinson, George (1862) <u>The Five Great Monarchies of Ancient Eastern Wolrd</u>. Vol 1. London: John Murray

Roux, Georges (1964) <u>Ancient Iraq</u>. London: George Allen& Unwin Limited

Smith, A.D (2010) <u>Nationalism</u>. Cambridge: Polity Press

Tabari, Abu-Jaffer Muhammad. (2007) <u>The History of al-Ṭabari</u>. Edited by Ehsan Yar-Shater. New York: University of New York Press.

Tate, G.p (1973) <u>The Kingdom of Afghanistan-A Historical Sketch</u>. Karachi: Indus Publications

Thapar, Romila (1977) <u>A History of India</u>, Vol.1.London: Penguin Books

Thomas de Marga. (1893) <u>The Book of Governors</u>. Translated by E. A. W. Budge. London: Gilbert and Rivington.

Toynbee, Arnold J (1978) <u>A Study of History</u>. London: Oxford University Press, PP 45-46

Waheed, Sheikh A (1955) <u>The Kurds and Their Country</u>. Lahore: Publishers United Limited

Wilkins, W.J (1974) <u>Hindu Mythology</u>. London: Rowman & Littlefield

Yu. V. Gankovsky (1971) <u>The Peoples of Pakistan</u>, Nauka, Moscow,1971 p 146

INDEX

Printed in the United States
By Bookmasters